The
Encyclopedic
Dictionary
of
CRIMINOLOGY

George E. Rush, Ph.D.

Sam Torres, Ph.D.

COPPERHOUSE PUBLISHING COMPANY
901-5 Tahoe Blvd.
Incline Village, Nevada 89451
(702) 833-3131 • Fax (702) 833-3133
e-mail info@copperhouse.com
http://www.copperhouse.com/copperhouse

Your Partner in Education
with
"QUALITY BOOKS AT FAIR PRICES"

The Encyclopedic Dictionary of Criminology

Library of Congress Catalog Number 97-67723
ISBN 0-942728-83-1 Paper Text Edition

2 3 4 5 6 7 8 9 10

Printed in the United States of America.

DEDICATION

To my children, Susan and Michael, and their children, Sarah, Chelsea and Chad.

George Rush

To my wife, Chris, who is the balancing force in my life. And to my daughter, Rikki, who lights it up.

Sam Torres

PREFACE

A review of the sources used to compile this *Encyclopedic Dictionary of Criminology* will attest to the attention and scope this topic has received from scholars within the broad field of criminology and criminal justice. By all means, this *Encyclopedic Dictionary* is not a conclusive nor a definitive collection. We have, however, attempted to serve the student a selective "cliff note" approach to the definitions of crime, the theories of crime, and related causal theory. We have included major contributors to the study of criminology which span or encompass many interacting disciplines... none of which hold the singular or definitive answer to the definition of crime, causal factors of deviance or problems associated with crime.

Criminological theories tend to build upon each other, contradict, overlap, and have a propensity for related theories to be called by various titles. It is no wonder as to why the teaching of criminological theory is a very challenging undertaking. It is towards this end that this book is directed.

A mastery of the terms and concepts associated with criminological theory is critical if the student and practitioner are to appreciate the etiology of crime and delinquency. The two major schools of crime causation theory, classical and positivist, each branch into a myriad of sub-theories, terms, and concepts which can easily confuse and overwhelm the student and layperson attempting to understand a particular criminal act. While many criminology textbooks include a glossary containing the major theories and theorists, they do not typically provide a detailed explanation and/or definition of the numerous subconcepts and terms utilized within the theory itself.

The Encyclopedic Dictionary of Criminology is intended to provide a quick reference to anyone seeking to understand the field of criminal justice—student, instructor, practitioner, layperson or administrator. While not exhaustive, this book is a meticulous effort to provide a detailed source of the most frequently used terms and concepts associated with criminological theory. Since criminological theory forms the basis of public policy, it is essential that students, practitioners, and the general public grasp an awareness of the diverse explanations as to why people commit the crimes they do and why government does what it does in an attempt to control criminal behavior.

The Encyclopedic Dictionary of Criminology provides the student of criminology and criminal justice with concise, yet comprehensive, definitions of key names and concepts. It will be an invaluable aid, not only for examinations, but also in providing people with an understanding of key concepts as they prepare research papers and review related literature.

George E. Rush, Ph.D.
and
Sam Torres, Ph.D.

INTRODUCTION

Criminology

Definition

The study of crime and criminals is the province of the field of criminology. As the Late Edwin Sutherland wrote in his classic work *Principles of Criminology* (1939:1): "Criminology is the body of knowledge regarding crime as a social phenomenon. It includes within its scope the processes of making laws, of breaking laws, and of reacting toward the breaking of laws." Although Sutherland's definition of criminology is commonly accepted and widely quoted, it is not quite accurate because it declares that the study of crime is solely focused on social factors. In fact, the study of crime by criminologists has encompassed several fields of knowledge that are not primarily social in nature.

It is also necessary to add that criminology has been generally defined as the *scientific* study of crime and criminals. Thus, not all those who comment on crime and criminals (such as forensic experts, lawyers, judges, and those who work in the criminal justice system) are criminologists. This distinction of a scientific approach to the subject is, however not as simple as it seems. There are scholars who consider themselves criminologists and yet do not embrace the scientific method. While these scholars are often Marxist or radical in their orientation, the key element is their denial of objectivity and quantification in research. Instead, they generally practice a methodology that studies crime and criminals from a dynamic, historical perspective. Further, these scholars usually focus on the "making of laws" and "reaction to the breaking of laws" rather than on the actual behavior of the lawbreaker. A few scholars, known as phenomenologists, study the meaning of behavior, rather than the subjects above.

As a final note on the definition of criminology, the terms *crime* and *criminal* are not as clear as they might seem. There has been much debate about what constitutes crime and criminals. Some have argued that the definition of crime is fully a legal matter: that is, if something is prohibited by law it is then and only then a crime. Others answer that because the laws are not really concerned with behavior itself, a legal definition does not provide a clear-cut focus for behavioral distinctions. The act of taking a life, for example, is not necessarily murder because states perform executions and nations go to war. They suggest that a social definition more tuned to deviance, in all of its forms, is a better approach. Yet other scholars point out that if a crime or deviant act is not noticed, then for all intents and purposes the act as well is deemed not to have occurred, and the individual involved is not defined/labeled criminal or deviant. Thus, the legal or social definitions of crime and criminals capture only those acts and persons to whom we react. This problem makes it difficult to talk of *criminals* and *non-criminals* and obscures the subject matter of the field.

Disciplinary Focus

Criminology is generally understood to be an offspring of the discipline of sociology. Although this is arguably the case, such a statement slights both the history of criminology and the various disciplines that comprise the breadth of the field. At one time or another, the disciplines of philosophy, history, anthropology, psychology, psychiatry, medicine, biology, genetics, endocrinology, neurochemistry, political science, economics, social work, jurisprudence, geography, urban planning, architecture, and statistics have all played prominent roles in the development of criminological theory and research. Since the 1930s, however, sociology has been the primary source of academic training for most criminologists. There have been very few academic departments of criminology in the United States and most of the scholarly preparation of criminologists has taken place in sociology departments. Nevertheless, in spite of this sociological focus, it should be recognized that criminology is characterized by a relative integration of materials from several disciplines. The advent and rise, through the last three decades, of the multidisciplinary field of criminal justice has challenged sociology as the training ground for criminology, and many criminologists are now either working in, or receiving their academic training from, criminal-justice departments. This movement promises to more directly integrate sociological criminology with other disciplines.

Within the general discipline of criminology lie several interest areas. In their more general forms they are allied with such fields as philosophy of law, sociology of law, sociology of deviance, penology/ corrections, police science, administration and demography. It is possible, then, to identify oneself as a criminologist and yet spend an entire career working within a relatively small areas of the field, such as policing.

Criminology in Academia

Because the discipline is so closely allied with sociology, there were very few criminology departments in the colleges and universities of America through the end of the 1960s. In fact, the most common way to enter the criminological field was to take a degree in sociology with a specialization in criminology. Until approximately 1970, only three major schools, University of California at Berkeley, Florida State University, and University of Maryland, had doctoral programs in criminology (the oldest related program, Michigan State University, was chiefly a police administration program). The count of schools offering criminology doctorates stands today at four. The program at Berkeley has been lost, having been phased out in the mid-1970s. Two new programs expressly titled as criminology degrees are now at the University of Delaware and Indiana University of Pennsylvania. The current approach seems to be the creation of doctoral programs in criminal justice, and there are now some dozen or so of those programs. In truth, there is now little distinction between criminology and criminal-justice doctoral programs.

The Development of Criminology

Criminology, as a generic form of study relating to crime and criminals, can be traced far back into history. It is only recently, however, that a systematic study developed. Perhaps the best estimate of the "birth" of criminology lies with the rise of the European Classical Period in the eighteenth century. The real thrust of the period was not so much the study of the criminal, but the systems of justice themselves. With relatively capricious and arbitrary laws in effect, the writers of the day (Montesquieu, Voltaire, Beccaria, Bentham) criticized the systems of justice and proposed massive reform. Referred to as the

Classical School of criminology, the ideas of these reformers became the basis for today's criminal law and justice systems, and originated the modern concept of deterrence.

In the nineteenth century, the study of crime and criminals began in earnest. Quetelet in France, Guerry in Belgium, and Mayhew in England were studying and mapping the distribution of crimes in what were the first real studies using so-called social statistics. Another group of people, under the leadership of Gall and Spurzheim, were engaged in the study of phrenology (the relationship of skull configuration—as an indication of brain structure—to behavior) and produced some of the first scientific studies of criminals. The generally accepted beginning of scientific criminology, however, occurred in the 1870s with the work of an Italian physician, Cesare Lombroso.

Drawing on the positive science methods of the day (thus the generic name "the Positive School"), Lombroso's work on the relationship between physical features, personality, and criminals led to theories of a "born" criminal and spurred both genetic and hereditary studies. It was during this period that the term criminology itself came into popular usage. Followed by two other Italians, Ferri and Garofalo, Lombroso's work was extended into the arena of social and environmental factors. With the rise of sociology as a discipline in the 1890s, scientific criminology expanded under a number of fronts.

The first two decades of the twentieth century saw an assortment of criminological explanations rise, most notably the social varieties, the emotional/psychoanalytic, and the combined product of then new intelligence testing and heredity research. By the 1920s, sociological studies were in full swing and the Sociology Department of the University of Chicago began to dominate criminology. The major explanations of criminality became tied to the transmission of values from one person to another, especially in areas that were culturally different and socially disorganized. In addition, statistical studies that placed crime and delinquency in particular areas of the city became popular.

By the 1940s, criminology had become concerned with the effect of social conditions on people in general and began an examination of the relationship among social structure, social class, and crime. Commonly known as "structural functionalist" theories, their focus was on differing rates of criminality or delinquency among groups of people in society. This approach held sway until the 1960s, when criminology, along with the rest of society, became concerned with civil rights and liberal political issues. The dominant theme of this period was quite reminiscent of a return to the old Classical School with its emphasis on justice and equality before law. Concerns shifted away from the criminal and toward the way in which the criminal-justice system reacted to and processed people.

Following the federal government's crusade and "war" against crime during the late 1960s and early 1970s, which culminated with the creation of the Law Enforcement Assistance Administration (now the National Institute of Justice), criminology became much more concerned with studying the criminal justice system itself. Under the aegis of LEAA funding, criminologists examined the operation of the police, the courts, and correctional systems with an eye to evaluating effectiveness. Also of concern was the treatment of victims and the measurement of crime, both which were blended into a new area of interest known as *victimology*. Because the discipline of criminal justice was also coming into its own during this period, the two fields began a merger, if not in fact, then in substance. The discipline of criminology is today quite difficult to distinguish from that of criminal justice.

Major Forms of Criminology

Although it is difficult to categorize criminology, one method is to distinguish among the study of the causes of criminality, the study of rates of criminality, and the study of the criminal-justice system as it operates. The first, with its focus on explaining behavior, is referred to as etiology or determinism. However, criminology generally concerns itself with the etiology (origins) of criminal behavior, while criminal justice is engaged in explaining the operation of the three components that make up the criminal justice system—police, courts, and corrections. The study of rates focuses on the prevalence and incidence of criminality and is called epidemiology. The third area of interest is more divergent than the other two and is composed of such aspects as punishment philosophies, penology, and policing.

Etiological criminology has contributed to an understanding of both criminal behavior (and deviance in general) and the presence of crime in society. Explanations have been generally of two types: processual and structural. The processual variety of theories attempts to explain how people *become* criminals and/or come to commit criminal acts. These theories are most often psychological or social psychological in orientation and usually deal with individual motivation and behavior. Because of the complexity of individual events, processual theories are sometimes only applicable to specific types of crime. Structural theories, on the other hand, are those that focus on the effect of society (and its institutions) on people in the aggregate and explain why different groups have different crime rates. As a result, structural theories are usually sociological in tone. It is theories of this type that have been the most successful in making sense out of crime in society, but they do not tell us which *individuals* will commit crimes.

Epidemiological criminology has given us an understanding of how (and sometimes why) rates of crime vary across classes of people or across time and space. We have learned, for example, that certain classes of people are more likely to be arrested for crimes (that is, they have higher crime rates). Further, we know that rates of crime vary with particular environmental conditions and geographic areas. Epidemiology also entails the study of the incidence of crime under various conditions, be they economic, social, or political. Criminologists have tracked the amount of crime across different types of political structures and in different economic times. They are currently very concerned with the amount of victimization and fear of crime in society.

Criminology that studies the criminal-justice system provides us with information on the way the system works, how closely reality matches our ideals, and alternatives that might reconcile the two. This type of criminology is perhaps best referred to as the study of the "system in action." This form of studying the various components of the criminal-justice system is in contrast to examinations of formal structure and is characterized by a study of the informal. In short, it focuses on the way things really work, not the way they are supposed to work. Thus, criminologists working in this area have studied the operation of police departments, the relationships between police and citizens, bail systems, plea bargaining, and the social structure of prisons, to name but a few of the areas of interest. Finally, for lack of a better classification, we can also place those criminologists who are interested in punishment theories within this category. Some current issues in this area are the death penalty, selective incapacitation, career criminals, and the construction of sentencing guidelines.

Relationship Between Criminology and Police Science

Along with the rise of academic criminology in the United States came the field of police science. Actually, police science departments preceded criminology departments in the colleges and universities. Although often difficult to distinguish from each other, police science departments usually focus more on the technical aspects of policing: administration, management, crime analysis, and the "doing" of law enforcement. Criminology, when it deals with the police province, more often uses the "system in action" focus. Thus, criminological approaches to the problem of policing are apt to be sociological in nature and to focus on informal structures and relationships.

Contribution of Criminology to Police Work

Because it is difficult to separate early criminology from early police science, one may argue that some of the first scientific contributions may have come from either source. Nonetheless, a review of the first three decades of the *Journal of Criminal Law and Criminology* suggests that much of contemporary policing was developed from early twentieth-century research. Articles include training, personnel selection, psychological testing, the use of technology, fingerprinting, and so forth. Obviously, the various techniques of crime analysis have their origins in early work on crime statistics.

On a more contemporary front, the criminological work of Egon Bittner, Albert Reiss, Jerome Skolnick, and Peter Manning has found its way into police training and community relations work. Similarly, the work of political scientist James Q. Wilson, who some view as a criminologist, has also had an effect on police administration practices. The products of civil disobedience research and victimization studies have changed police selection processes and created an emphasis on education. More recent work by criminologists has led many police departments to rethink several of their basic conceptions. Kelling's Kansas City Preventive Patrol Experiment caused police departments nationwide to rethink their patrol procedures. Several response time studies suggested that immediate response to all citizen calls was not necessary and that response time was not as critical to making an arrest as was thought. Sherman and Berk's research on response to spousal assault calls led to changes in response and arrest policies for disturbance calls. Studies by the Rand Corporation and the Police Executive Research Foundation on detective work and crime solving resulted in patrol officers being given more responsibility in the investigative process and in new ways to screen cases. A criminological theory, routine activities, has precipitated a new analytical approach to locating crime, known as "hot spots." And, finally, Herman Goldstein"s work, particularly his book *Problem-Oriented Policing*, influenced many police department to give up traditional policing for variations on community policing.

In short, criminology is not focused on the police by any means but it has had a profound effect, which ranges from the Classical School's reform of criminal-justice operation and philosophy to the techniques used by police departments today. With the current emphasis on system examination and efficiency research, it is only reasonable to assume that police and criminologists will continue to build on their relationship. Indeed, among the components of today's criminal-justice system it is the police who are relying most heavily on criminological research to make substantial changes in basic structure and methods of operating.

Frank Williams

Frank Williams, Ph.D.
Department of Criminal Justice
California State University, San Bernardino

A

absolute deterrent. A crime control strategy developed to eradicate a certain type of criminality.

Academy of Criminal Justice Sciences (ACJS). An organization of academicians and practitioners joined by the common purpose to further the discipline of criminal justice.

accomplice. A person who helps another to commit a crime.

Ackers, Ronald (1939-) Best known for this theory outlined in his book *Deviant Behavior: A Social Learning Approach* (1977), wherein he describes how people learn deviant behavior through operant conditioning. That is, behavior is controlled by its consequences. If the behavior is reinforced or rewarded, the behavior will probably be repeated. If the behavior is punished, the probability that the behavior will be repeated is decreased. Another important concept in this theory is behavior modeling, which involves imitation of the behavior of significant persons (parents, teachers, peers) who are respected or admired.

acting out. A form of defense mechanism or a procedure in psychotherapy. It takes the form of directly displaying problems and conflicts, especially those involving aggression and hostility, in overt behavior rather than experiencing them internally and displaying them indirectly or symbolically.

actus reus. A prohibited behavior required before a person can be charged with a crime; the act itself, independent of motive or intent.

Addams, Jane (1860-1910) Founded the Chicago Hull House in the 1890s. This was a shelter for runaway youths and others in need of food, clothing and shelter.

adjudication. The judicial process of finding a defendant guilty of a crime.

Adler, Alfred (1870-1937). Austrian psychiatrist. He worked with Sigmund Freud but disagreements with Freud, particularly over his theory of compensation for inferiority feelings, and greater emphasis on the social aspects of neurosis, led Adler to develop his own rival approach, called *individual psychology.* Adler's theories of personality emphasized the significance of social influences and goal striving. Adler held that each individual from his early capacities, limitations, and experiences develops a unique style of life that is predominantly social in orientation. While every person has the same ultimate goal of superiority, or positive self-esteem, there are innumerable individual ways of striving for this goal. Maladjustment occurs when one has drawn false conclusions about the world and himself and consequently adopts a faulty life-style that is primarily self-centered and defensive.

adversary system. The American courts are organized on the principle that the prosecution (the state) and the defense (the attorney for the accused) shall engage in legal "combat" on equal terms before a neutral judge.

aging-out phenomenon (theory). A concept which holds that offenders commit less crime as they get older because they have less strength, initiative, stamina, and mobility. James Q. Wilson and Richard Hernstein have argued that an aging-out process is responsible for the decline of crime among the elderly.

aggravated assault. (*See:* assault).

aggression. The theory of aggression remains one of the most challenging areas of criminological study because of the elusiveness of an adequate definition of the term. Some researchers have applied it to any act that inflicts pain or suffering on another individual; others feel that a proper definition must include some notion of intent to do harm. Still others use a situational definition, so that what might be described as aggression in one context but might not be considered as such in others. Yet others, contend that only the outcome of the act or "harm" should be considered.

alcoholism. A behavioral disorder characterized by habitual and excessive drinking of alcoholic beverages that disrupts daily social and occupational functioning and physical health. There are numerous explanations put forth to explain alcohol including biological, psychological, social, and rational-choice theories. In addition, integrated theories attempt to explain alcoholism utilizing a combination of theoretical constructs.

The causes of alcoholism are still a matter of speculation. Extant theories cite such factors as meeting unmet dependency needs, fulfilling the need for power, and reducing tension and psychological pain through the use of alcohol. Cultural factors play a role because the prevalence of alcoholism in different cultures varies considerably. There is also the possibility that alcoholism is partially associated with genetically inherited physiological and biochemical anomalies. One possible inherited biochemical predisposing factor may be that people at high risk for alcoholism metabolize alcohol at a higher rate than people at low risk, so that the former consume more alcohol.

alienation. To be alienated means to be estranged from one's society. One of the main causes of alienation is rapid social change, which in turn, accounts for at least three different types of alienated behavior. The first type is man's inability to adapt to rapid change. The second is related to it, in that social change has produced a trend toward urban living, resulting in depersonalized living relationships. Third, social upheaval has fostered doubts and finally disagreements about all types of behavioral standards. The result has been widespread uncertainty about traditional values.

alien conspiracy theory. A position that organized crime was imported by Europeans and that criminal organizations restrict their membership to individuals of their own ethnic origins.

alloplastic adaption. A form of adjustment which results from changes in the environment surrounding a person.

alternative sanctions. Generally referred to as intermediate sanctions. These punishments are more severe than straight probation but less severe than prison. Examples, of alternative sanctions include electronic monitoring, community service, fines, restitution, halfway placement and drug testing.

anarchist theory of punishment. This concept contains the beliefs that modern society is based on structured power relationships and that deviant behavior is a direct product of fitting human relationships into hierarchical rules. This belief further asserts that the current punishment system preserves the power system while reducing human capacity and ability for cooperation.

androgens. Refers to the male sex hormones. Testosterone is the principal androgen found in males.

anomie. A concept first formulated by Emile Durkheim to describe a state of normlessness in which social control of individual behavior has become ineffective. The concept provides the reference point for his critical analysis of the problems of modern society.

Preconditions. Anomie is apt to arise when certain preconditions for the individual's successful integration into society are lacking. These preconditions are that individual behavior should be governed by social norms, that the norms themselves should form a consistent and coherent value system, and that each individual should be morally involved with others so that permissible boundaries of individual self-indulgence are clearly demarcated. If social norms break down, if there is a conflict of norms, or if individuals are detached from their moral relationships to their fellows, anomie will tend to result. Lacking any source of restraint, the person will tend to satisfy his or her own appetites, only to discover that they are insatiable; goals constantly recede and always appear unfulfilled. The result of this normlessness is a deep psychological disturbance at the individual level, lack of cohesion, and if individual anomie is widespread, disorder at the societal level.

The Role of Social Change. Anomie, according to Durkheim, is associated particularly with times of rapid or major social change. As societies grow more complex, a form of "organic solidarity" develops in which social cohesion is based on the interdependence of the highly individuated members. The growth of individualism is an inevitable result of the growth of the division of labor, and individualism can develop only at the expense of the common sentiments and beliefs. As a result, the belief system becomes more generalized, with greater scope for individual interpretations and differences.

Anomie and Social Change. In his influential study of suicide, Durkheim applied his notion of anomie to a contrast between suicide in traditional and modern societies. The dominant type of suicide in traditional societies, he determined, as "altruistic"—that is, an act committed in recognition of social norms so powerful that they overrode the individual will to live. In modern societies, however, "anomic" suicide is the dominant form. This suicide arises from the particular social structure, whatever its individual genesis, and is commonly found in times of social dislocation, which produce fluctuations in the fortunes of individuals, or groups. An example would be the individual who decides that "life is meaningless" and kills himself.

New Views. Durkheim was not a reactive conservative who looked for the reintroduction of older norms; he fully recognized that they were no longer appropriate for a society based on organic solidarity. His diagnosis was that a new and more appropriate system of beliefs and values was needed, one that would legitimate the cult of the individual and also provide the necessary restraint on unfettered individual desires by making those urges subject to normative regulation once more.

anthropology. The science founded on the study of mankind and its development in relation to its physical, mental, and cultural history. It is a comprehensive science, embracing other disciplines such as criminology, biology, physiology, psychology, comparative anatomy, and sociology. Specifically, anthropology may be considered the science of man's natural history in relation to his physical character, rather than the general science of man. Anthropological theories simply attempt to explain behavior generally, and criminal behavior specifically, primarily through the influence of human culture. Physical anthropology, a subdiscipline, attempts, to explain behavior through the study of human biology, human evolution, or human genetics.

anthropophagy. A sexual offense related to the eating of human flesh (cannibalism) and the drinking of human blood (vampirism).

antisocial personality. Used synonymously with psychopathy and sociopathy. A pervasive pattern of personality disorder characterized by a lack of guilt feelings, inability to empathize with others, outward charm, a high intelligence, an inability to learn from experiences, self-centeredness, an inability to defer gratification, and disregard for the rights of others. This disorder also includes the traits of being callous and cynical with an inflated and arrogant self appraisal. In view of these traits, the antisocial personality is at high risk for deviant behavior. Biological, psychological, and sociological theories have been postulated to explain causative factors for this particular disorder.

apathy-indifference. In an increasingly urban and impersonal society, apathy has become a problem of growing concern to social scientists. On March 14, 1964 at 3:20 A.M., 28-year-old Kitty Genovese returned home from work in Queens County, NY, a borough of New York City. A man stabbed her and began to sexually assault her. She screamed and lights came on in the apartment houses. For the next 25 minutes, the attacker stalked, assaulted, and stabbed her until she eventually died just before 3:50

A.M. Although 37 witnesses heard her screams for help and watched the assault, the first call to the police did not occur until some minutes after her death. Two factors are known to contribute to the origins of such remarkable indifference: anonymity and deindividuation play large roles in creating a climate of indifference. Studies of helping behavior, for example, show that as the number of witnesses to a help-requiring situation increases, the amount of helping that occurs decreases, and the time that passes before anyone offers help increases. Because the presence of others serves to increase the anonymity of the observers, it leads to diffusion of responsibility; no individual feels personally involved and each assumes someone else will help out. The second factor contributing to indifference is perceived loss of control. As individuals become convinced that they are less and less in charge of their own lives, their willingness to try to change things decreases.

appeal. A request by a higher court to review the decision of a lower court. Appeal can also reflect a petition by a person committed in a lesser court for a review of the case by an appeals (higher) court (by a writ of errors or *certiorari*). In the federal system the circuit court is considered an intermediate court of appeals, while the U.S. Supreme Court is the final court of appeals. State systems tend to be organized along similar lines. However, when an issue involves a constitutional question, such as is frequently the case in death-penalty cases, the appeal may move from the state to the federal system.

appellant. A party who has lost a case in a lower court and who is appealing the case to a higher court.

appellate courts. A higher court which has jurisdiction to reconsider the decision of a lower court (*See*: appeal).

Aquinas, St. Thomas (1224-1274). An Italian Dominican priest and theologian, Aquinas developed a complete moral system in which he analyzed the nature of the human acts of reasoning and will and related them to virtues and vices. He emphasized popular participation in government, the necessity of a well-ordered society, the advantages of a unified rule, and the evils of tyranny. His most important work was *Summa Theologica,* a systematic exposition of theology on philosophical principles.

argot. A specialized language that creates solidarity by differentiating a group from outsiders.

Aristotle (384-322 B.C.). A student of Plato, the Greek philosopher Aristotle wrote in one of his treaties, *Politics*, that the political community is the source and sustainer of human life. However, the highest good for man is found not in political life but in theoretical inquiry and contemplation of truth.

arraignment. The first stage of the judicial process, at which the indictment or information is read in open court and the defendant is requested to respond. The accused is also advised of his or her due-process rights and the issue of bail is decided.

arrest. The taking of a person into custody for violation of a criminal statute; the legal detainment of a person to answer for criminal charges.

arson. The intentional damaging or destruction or attempted damaging or destruction, by means of fire or explosives, of property without the consent of the owner, or of one's own property or that of another by fire or explosives with or without the intent to defraud.

assault. The unlawful, intentional inflicting, or attempted inflicting, of injury upon the person of another. The assault may be verbal. However, the term battery is used to represent the unlawful touching of a person. Aggravated assault is the result of the unlawful intentional inflicting of serious bodily injury or death by means of a deadly or dangerous weapon, with or without infliction of injury. Simple assault is the unlawful or intentional inflicting of less than serious or serious bodily injury or an attempt or threat to inflict bodily injury without a deadly or dangerous weapon.

assembly-line justice. Comparison of the criminal justice process to an assembly line because of its mechanized approach to moving cases along.

assimilation. Complete or partial adaption of one culture by another, in which one culture might take on some characteristics of the other.

atavism. Derived from a Latin term *atavus* meaning "ancestor." A positivist school theory of criminal behavior, developed by Lombroso and other evolutionists in the post-Darwinian era. It postulates that criminality diminishes in the evolutionary development of humanity, and that its appearance as a biological predilection in some persons is a hereditary throwback on the evolutionary scale. (*See:* Lombroso, Cesare)

Attention Deficit Disorder (ADT). This disorder is characterized by impulsive behavior, hyperactivity, and an inappropriate lack of concentration. This condition is associated with poor school performance and a lack of response to discipline.

Auburn System. (Congregate hard labor plan). The organizing principle for prisoners begun in Auburn, New York, in 1821 and still prevails. It emphasized common activities, external discipline, hard labor, and forced rehabilitation. Differed from Pennsylvania system in that the Auburn of New York system allowed inmates to work together (congregate) in silence during the day.

Augustus, John (1785-1859). The noted founder of the probation system in America. Called the "father of probation," John Augustus was a Boston boot maker who was the first to invent a system which he called probation. In 1841, at the age of 57, Augustus was in a Boston court and observed a man being arraigned for public drunkenness. John Augustus requested that the court allow the man to be released to his supervision. He thus became the first probation officer, with supervision of minor offenders. In 1852, he published *A Report of the Labors of John Augustus.*

authoritarian personality. A group of traits that include a high level of conformity, blind obedience to authority, exaggerated control of feelings and impulses and rigid thinking patterns. Persons who possess these traits rigidly follow conventional values, identify with authority figures and are generally antagonistic toward minority groups. The syndrome was first recognized in 1950 by Adorno, Frenkell-Brunswik, and others in the book *The Authoritarian Personality.* (*See*: f scale)

autoplastic adaptation. A form of adjustment which results from changes within a person.

avoidant personality disorder. Behavioral traits include a pattern of social inhibitions and feelings of inadequacy which are manifested by seeking to avoid or withdraw from socially threatening situations.

B

bail. A form of pretrial release whereby defendants post bond to guarantee their appearance at a trial. The accused may post the entire amount or pay a portion usually 10% to a bondsman who then posts the bond. The 10% becomes the fee for services. The bail is forfeited if the defendant does not appear for trial.

bail bondsman. A person who posts bail for a defendant for a fee (usually 10%).

Bail Reform Act of 1984. Legislation enacted by Congress to speed the release of nonviolent offenders who pose a minimal threat to the community. However, this act also allows judges to order defendants confined pending further proceedings if a finding is made that they pose a danger to the community or pose a high risk of fleeing the jurisdiction of the court. Preventive detention is the term used to refer to keeping an accused in custody.

banishment. Historically this was a form of punishment whereby a person was exiled from a community for a specific time or for life. During the colonial period, England transported large numbers of felons to the American colonies (*See:* transportation).

battered woman syndrome. The physical and emotional effects of deliberate and continuous beating of a female by her spouse or live-in partner. Wife abuse is not a recent or new phenomenon. There are statements in Frankish common law that indicate that a man has the right to discipline his slaves, his children, and his wife. In some cultures it was not a crime to murder one's wife. Battered woman syndrome is so named because, in the opinion of some experts, the condition does not describe only the woman, but refers to a collection of characteristics that appear in both the man and the woman. Wife battering tends to be episodic, with sometimes long periods of relative peace between episodes. The battered woman syndrome is seen by some as an ailment of a marriage.

battery. A common law crime consisting of the unlawful and unwelcome intentional touching, beating or inflicting harm on another.

Beccaria, Cesare (1738-1794). An Italian philosopher who is considered to be the "father of classical criminology." Beccaria was considered a reformer in 18th century Italy. He argued against the harsh penalties of his day that included torture, death, and an absence of due process. Crime, according to Beccaria, was the result of free will or choice that could be deterred with punishment proportionate to the severity of the crime (*See*: classical school).

Becker, Howard S. (1928-). American sociologist noted for his contributions to the methodology of participant observation, the sociology of deviance, and the sociology of art.

Becker's work on deviance is probably his best known. Following in the tradition of Edwin Sutherland, he demonstrated that deviant behavior is learned through contact with particular social groups in which that behavior is routinely practiced. "Deviance" is thus considered to be a result of group membership, not an individual aberration.

He went on to suggest a labeling theory. Behavior that society regards as "deviant" is behavior that some "social control agents" have been successful in labeling as deviant. What all types of deviance do have in common is the application of rules by which they can be punished. Labeling theory has some similarity to conflict theory in that both attribute the creation of laws and deviance to those in positions of power who seek to control their own interests. Criminologists study ways in which rules are constructed and the sanctions applied to various groups and activities.

Bedau, Hugo Adam (1926-). An opponent of the death penalty, he along with Michael Radelet he authored *Miscarriages of Justice in Potentially Capital Cases* (1987), wherein he claimed that there have been about 350 wrongful convictions in the 20th century, of which approximately 23 have led to execution. In addition to the 23 that were wrongfully executed, 128 of the wrongfully convicted served over six years in prison, 39 served more than 16 years, and eight died while incarcerated. In 1974, Bedau argued that victimless crimes should be removed from the criminal justice system.

Behaviorism. A school of thought within the discipline of psychology that focuses on observable behavior. Behaviorists believe it serves little purpose to focus on motives, attitudes or mental processes that are difficult to decipher. Instead, behaviorists attempt to modify specific behaviors that are causing pain and discomfort to the individual.

behavior modification. A method of treating offenders, based on the belief that all behavior is learned and that socially acceptable behavior can be learned as a replacement for deviant behavior. There are two basic types of behavior modification: (1) classical conditioning, spawned by the

Russian physiologist Ivan Petrovitch Pavlov in the 1920s, which has usually been associated with negative reinforcers, such as shock treatments and deprivation of privileges for undesirable behavior; and (2) operant conditioning, which is best exemplified in the research and writings of B.F. Skinner.

In criminal justice, behavior modification is frequently associated with token economy treatment strategies utilized in juvenile institutions. With this type of program, delinquents are rewarded with "tokens" when they exhibit positive behavior (like performing well in school and complying with the unit rules). These tokens are then exchanged for privileges such as extra food, preferred housing, early release, or positions of leadership. Like most other treatment programs, maintaining the positive behavior is difficult once the juvenile is returned to the negative influences of his or her home or neighborhood. The distinction between the two theories appears to be that classical conditioning seeks to modify basic emotional responses, while operant conditioning seeks to modify behavior by using reinforcement and punishment strategies.

Bentham, Jeremy (1748-1832). British founder of the Utilitarian school of philosophy, also a research methodologist, jurist, and applied social scientist. Repelled by the gross inequalities of English life, he became a radical reformer whose arguments and recommendations remain forceful today.

Bentham sought to apply the precise language and methods of the psychical sciences to the social sciences and to apply social-science knowledge to the rational improvement of the condition of men. He successfully sought improved subsistence levels, greater abundance, increased security, and more equality for the English people. Thus, in effect, he defined the major goals of the welfare state as well as the means of achieving them. His disciples moved through Parliament such measures as the Public Health Act, the Railway Regulation Act, the Poor Law, and the Education Act. They combined the separate courts of law and equity, reformed penal codes, and extended democracy with the Reform Bill of 1832. Bentham is known for his "Hedonistic Calculus," which sought to quantify the necessary punishment needed to exceed the benefit (pleasure) derived of a criminal act and thus deter criminality.

Bertillon, Alphonse (1853-1914). French criminologist considered the creator of forensic science. He devised the first scientific system for the identification of a person based upon measurements of the body. Bertillon also developed a system of forensic photography using standardized photos of full face and profile.

bias. A predisposition based on marginal evidence or unsubstantiated evidence, which will often be used to confirm a particular opinion, point of view, or issue.

Binet, Alfred (1857-1911). French psychologist and educator. Binet was a pioneer in the study of individual differences in abilities and introduced intelligence tests that became widely used in Europe and the United States. He was asked by the French government to develop an objective method for distinguishing between retarded and normal children so that they could be given special instruction. In collaboration with Theodore Simon, he developed the first scales for measuring intelligence. He made use of simple materials, such as pictures and small objects, in devising these tests. Binet claimed that he was measuring "general mental ability" rather than specific achievement or learning. Items on the scale were placed according to the particular age group for which they were best suited (from three-year old to adult). Binet also developed the concept of "mental age," which relates to a person's level of intellectual functioning, regardless of actual age. Binet's efforts influenced Lewis M. Terman, an American psychologist who published the *Stanford Revision of the Binet-Simon Scale* (1916). This was for many years the most popular intelligence test in the United States.

biocriminology. (Also referred to as "biological determinism/ positivism). A relatively new subdiscipline of criminology, developed in the past two decades, which attempts to explain criminal behavior by referring to biological and genetic factors that predispose some individuals to commit criminal acts (*See*: biological determinism).

biographical method. A research strategy in which the experiences of a single individual are examined in detail.

biological determinism. The theory that certain qualities inherent in an organism cause its behavior. In this view the substantive concerns of social science are eliminated or at least enormously subordinated. A number of theories of human development are biologically deterministic. Cesare Lombroso claimed that those who become criminal are degenerate and animalistic, with identifiable atavisms—regressive, apelike qualities (*See*: biocriminology).

biological factors (hormones). Biosocial theories assert that there is an association between abnormal levels of male sex hormones (androgens) and violence. Female hormones (estrogen and progesterone) have been given to male sex offenders in an attempt to decrease their sexual impulses. The major area of hormonal study has been with the male hormone testosterone. Biosocial theorists suggest that abnormally high levels of testosterone contribute to elevated levels of aggression. Some studies have found that male offenders who commit crimes of violence tend to have higher levels of testosterone. In his 1993 book, *The Moral Sense*, James Q. Wilson presents a discussion on hormones, enzymes, and neurotransmittters that he feels may explain criminal behavior. Hormones, he explains, are the primary reason that the vast majority of crimes are committed by males who are biologically more aggressive than females.

biosocial criminology. A contemporary resurgence of presociological and nonsociological explanations of the sources of crime. According to these theories, the ultimate causes of criminal behavior are found in the physical and biological makeup of the individual offender. Although these theories purport to integrate biological and social factors, biological factors tend to predominate as explanations of criminality.

birth cohort. A group consisting of all individuals within a population born in the same year. The most famous birth cohort in criminology is Wolfgang's cohort.

Bittner, Egon (1921-) Scholar and professor of Brandeis University. Among other findings, he concluded in his academic study *The Functions of Police in Modern Society: A Review of Background Factors, Current Practices, and Possible Role Models* (1980) that patrol officers average about 10 arrests per month and only about three Part 1 index crime arrests per year. He also asserted that a highly-trained elite police force magnifies the danger of tyranny and that power in any form must be regulated and controlled.

blameworthiness. Culpability. Determined by examining the mitigating and aggravating factors present in a particular offense. Mitigating factors decrease blameworthiness while aggravating factors increase blameworthiness. Determining the degree of blameworthiness or culpability is critical because it determines the severity of the punishment to be administered by the court (*See*: behavior modification).

Bodin, Jean (1530-1596). A French philosopher who, in *Six Lives de la Republique*, attempted to construct a systematic, scientific approach to politics. He felt that the government should guide by the example of virtuous activity, which would eliminate corruption, and establish laws that would provide a majority of the people with good lives.

Bonger, Willem Adriaan (1876-1940). A Dutch criminologist credited with identifying criminology in the Netherlands as a separate field of science. His small classic, *An Introduction to Criminology*, was a great success. Even today, there is no other textbook that gives such a complete survey of criminology so compactly. Through this book and his doctoral thesis, *Criminality and Economic Conditions*, Bonger had great influence on American and English authors.

Bonneville, Arnould de Marsangy (1802-1894). An influential voice in the field of criminal and legislative reforms in France during the mid-19th century.

booking. The initial process of recording the name, address, and other pertinent information about a suspect arrested by the police, including the charge, arresting officers, and date of arrest. Fingerprints and a "mug shot" or photograph of the arrestee are also taken during the booking process.

boot camp. A recent correctional strategy or fad. Generally, considered an intermediate sanction wherein the offender is committed to a facility patterned after a recruit level or basic entry military training program. During the four-six month confinement, the inmate participates in a rigorous physical program that includes intense military training elements like the wearing of uniforms, utilizing a rank structure, and frequent drills. There is a strong emphasis on self-discipline and the range of programs offered include educational, vocational, therapeutic, and drug education and treatment. Almost all of these programs involve a period of intensive supervision upon release.

bourgeoisie. A class of people, in Marxist theory, that owns the means of production. Also referred to as the elite, affluent and powerful members of society that shape the criminal law.

Bovee, Marvin H. (1827-1888). Anti-capital punishment crusader who began his career as a Wisconsin legislator. His speeches and legislative labors resulted in various reforms.

Bradford, William (1721-1791). Bradford, termed the "Patriot Printer of 1776," was one of the early advocates of a Continental Congress. He was a member of the Sons of Liberty, a political rival of Benjamin Franklin, and an active reformer of the harsh British codes. As a major in the army, he became a hero of the Revolution.

Bristow, Benjamin Helm (1832-1896). An American lawyer, unionist, and federal official. As U.S. attorney in Kentucky, he fought the Ku Klux Klan. As U.S. Secretary of the Treasury, he crushed the Whiskey Ring.

Brockway, Zebulon E. (1827-1920). American penologist who began his career at the age of 21 as a clerk at the Wethersfield, CT, prison. Six years later, he became superintendent of the Monroe County Penitentiary in Rochester, NY, where he first experimented with ideas to make prisons more humane and rehabilitative. As the first superintendent of Elmira (NY) Reformatory in 1876, Brockway was responsible for the first use of the indeterminate sentence in the U.S., thereby introducing the use of parole. Brockway also implemented the rehabilitation strategies of classification and treatment programs. He was a charter member of the National Prison Association and was its president in 1898. His autobiography, *Fifty Years of Prison Service*, was published in 1912.

broken window syndrome. A public safety theory that neighborhoods deteriorate rapidly if initial cases of vandalism, such as broken windows or graffiti, are ignored by responsible agencies.

Bronner, Augusta. She and William Healy conducted a study in 1926 of delinquent boys and found that they were five to 10 times more apt to be subnormal in intelligence as compared with nondelinquent youth.

brothel. A house of prostitution. Brothels are illegal in most jurisdictions in the United States, except in several counties in Nevada.

brutalization effect. The belief that capital punishment encourages rather than discourages violent behavior. The execution itself, being violent and brutal, is thought to contribute to aggressive behavior.

burglary. Unlawful entry into any fixed structure, dwelling or dwelling-house, vehicle, or vessel used for regular residence, industry, or business, with or without force, with intent to commit a felony or larceny.

C

capital punishment. The execution of an offender who has committed a capital offense (murder). A significant element in classical rational choice and deterrence theories, which hold that the death penalty serves the purpose of deterrence, incapacitation and retribution.

career criminal. Also referred to as a chronic offender. A person who supports himself or herself through criminal activity. Although the number of convictions necessary to be considered a career criminal vary from jurisdiction to jurisdiction, three to four is common in most systems.

Cartographic School. An early school of thought seeking the causes of deviant behavior. The cartographic-geographic school studied the ecological facts of crime where it occurs. Fifty years before Cesare Lombroso expounded his physiological theories, Adolphe Quetelet in Belgium and A.M. Guerry in France were studying the phenomenon of crime, seeking to link it to sociological conditions in high-crime areas. From their studies they determined that crime proliferated in areas characterized by low social cohesion, weak family life, low economic status, physical deterioration of property, high population mobility, and various forms of personal demoralization. These variables influenced Lombroso in his later writings and are taken into account by almost all schools of thought today. (*See*: Quetelet; Lombroso).

case law. Judicial precedent generated as a by-product of the decisions that courts have made to resolve unique disputes, as distinguished from statutes and constitutions. Case law generally concerns facts; statutes and constitutions written in the abstract. (*See:* common law).

castration. In earlier times the removal of the testicles in the male offender for the crime of rape.

causation. The belief that crime and delinquency is determined by antecedent events. Causation presumes a relationship between two events in which the presence of one brings about the other. For example, the assumption in social structure theory that poverty contributes to delinquency.

caveat emptor. Latin for "let the buyer beware" that is often used to justify fraudulent behavior. The belief that it is the responsibility of the consumer to exercise caution in business transactions.

Chambliss, William J. (1933-). This conflict criminologist, along with Robert Seidman authored *Law, Order and Power,* which demonstrated how the criminal justice system operates to protect the rich and powerful. Chambliss noted that in the United States, freedom (capitalism) allows one group to make a profit over another group. The perpetuation of the existing justice system reflects a choice to support the existing economic and power structure that favors the rich. The freedom protected by the system of laws, according to Chambliss, is the freedom of those who can afford it. The law serves the interest of the rich and powerful at the expense of the poor.

charge. The formal allegation that a defendant has committed a particular offense or series of offenses. Charging instruments include, information, complaint, and indictment.

Chicago School. Shortened name for The Chicago School of Human Ecology (formerly School of Sociology) at the University of Chicago. It stressed the role of socioeconomic factors in causing crime, and saw crime as a phenomenon particular to certain areas of the city. Criminological textbooks generally included socioeconomics as one of the earliest social structural theories. Earlier, the Chicago School had been influenced by the cartographic school of crime research that flourished in the 1920s. Chicago School studies were important not only because of their substance, but also because they provided the earliest recognizable sociological and criminological research in the United States. The "concept of concentric circles or ecological zones," formulated by Chicago School sociologists, initially held that crime decreased zone by zone as one moved farther from the core of the city (*See:* Cartographic school).

chivalry hypothesis. This is a gender-based explanation for judicial leniency toward female offenders. It asserts that much of the criminality among females is not reported or hidden because of the protective and benevolent attitudes towards them individually and as a group by the criminal justice system.

chromosomes, XYY. Some scientific findings since 1961 have indicated that a number of males with an extra Y chromosome (XYY) have had histories of violent and antisocial behavior. There were different points of view about this unique genotype until 1968, when news stories focused on three convicted murderers (including Gary Gilmore) who reportedly had this chromosomal defect. (One of them was later shown to be normal in this respect.) Many geneticists doubt that the available evidence established a cause-and-effect relationship between such defects and deviant behavior. Research has largely discredited this theory by finding as many XYY men in the general population as in prison populations.

chronic offender. Marvin Wolfgang coined this term to refer to his Philadelphia cohort of delinquents who were arrested five or more times before age 18. Along with Thorsten Sellin and Robert Figlio, he found that the "chronic 6 percent" were responsible for a disproportionate amount of crime. This term is often used interchangeably with the concept of the *career criminal*.

civil law. Law that is not criminal, including tort, contract, and property law. The burden of proof required in a criminal proceeding is beyond a reasonable doubt, while the burden of proof in a civil proceeding is reduced to the preponderance of the evidence.

class conflict. Those who find themselves having differing interests or beliefs based on their level within a formal or informal class-structured society.

classical penal theory. The theory advanced by 18th-century jurists and philosophers, notably Beccaria (Italian), Bentham (English), and Feuerbach (German), holding that punishments for crimes should be imposed exactly according to the degree of seriousness of the offense. This theory was widely incorporated in penal laws and still operates in Europe and America in the majority of provisions for convicting and sentencing of criminals. In Europe the major deviation is the absence of the death penalty. In the United States, this theory has been the predominant influence on public policy since the late 1970s. It incorporates determinate sentencing, mandatory minimum sentencing, elimination of parole, and reduction of good time. The concept is associated with conservative politics.

Classical School. Associated with Cesare Bonesana, Marchese de Beccaria and developed in the eighteenth century, Classical School assumes that crime is a product of an individual's exercise of free will and that the administration of punishment equal to the harm it causes is the right of the state. This theory was later modified and called Neo-Classical Theory, which allowed for consideration of mitigating circumstances such as age and mental state. According to this theory, people are rational and weigh the benefits and costs of criminal behavior before acting. Also referred to as Rational Choice Theory, Just Deserts Theory, Anti-Determinism, Punishment Model, and Accountability Model. This school of thought is consistent with the goals of retribution, deterrence, and incapacitation (*See:* Beccaria).

classification. The separation of prisoners into various classes or custody groups depending on various elements, such as age, type of crime, danger, escape risk, or medical condition.

class system. A stratification or grouping of individuals in a society that may be forced together based on a particular factor like income, race, religion, or occupation.

Code of Hammurabi. The Babylonian Code of Hammurabi— discovered by the French in 1902—is the most famous of the Mespotamian codes to survive in its entirety. Certain of the code's legal phrases indicate that the Code (circa 1760 B.C.) was based on prior codes. It is generally regarded by historians as a moderate and humanitarian code for its period. (*See:* Mesopotamian laws and codes).

codified norms. Customs or norms that reflect accepted behavior passed as a law.

cognitive dissonance. This theory was developed by Leon Festinger. He postulated that an individual strives for internal harmony and consistency within so that the individual's attitudes, values, beliefs, and opinions are consonant with each other and with that person's behavior. It was noted that, although there is a consistency between cognitive elements, in some instances, inconsistency, or dissonance, occurs. An example would be a person who continues a habit known to be physically harmful. Another example would be a person who purchases something he or she did not really desire and then verbalizes the item's positive qualities or how happy he or she is to have purchased it in an attempt to develop internal mental harmony. This is an attempt to convince oneself and others that he or she really did want the item.

cognitive theory. A branch of psychology that focuses on the mental processes of individuals. The theory tends to focus on perceptual distortions of reality which create problems in relationships.

cohort. A group or class of people sharing certain significant social characteristics in common, such as sex, time, place of birth or demographics (*See*: birth cohort; cohort study).

cohort study. A research experiment examining the same group of people on a specific variable over a period of time (*See*: chronic offender).

collective action theory. Attempts to explain how and why individuals come together to pursue their joint interests at some times and places but not at others. A revival of interest in this theory occurred during the 1960s when workers and students in many countries around the world took to the streets together to demand social change. Three general approaches have been offered: one view holds that protests occur when the gap between the haves and the have-nots increases, making clear to those with fewer economic or political rights their subordinate position; other theorists argue that the oppressed must gain new organizational capacities to protest effectively, something more likely to happen when the disadvantaged first begin to improve their position; a third approach emphasizes divisions in the ruling elite as the source of opportunities for protest and cross-class alliances

Colquhoun, Patrick (1745-1820). A British magistrate who published *Treatise on the Police of the Metropolis*, a book that contained discussions of various forms of criminal behavior. He recommended a register of offenders, improved communication between city and rural magistrates, and the creation of a centralized, trained, vigilant, and active police body.

common law. Often called "Law of Customs" and was not codified in writing. Common law was a philosophy of law that has been adopted from England. Broadly, it holds that the law "is common" to all persons regardless of station, wealth, occupation or status. Common law consists of traits that aid the court in making decisions, as opposed to case law.

community-based corrections. A penological philosophy that emphasizes punishment and treatment in the community. It prevents destructive effects of imprisonment while facilitating reintegration into the community. Examples include group homes, halfway houses, work release programs, electronic monitoring, and parole.

community policing. A philosophical change in the basic strategy of policing that is geared towards "quality of life" issues. It relies on both police and citizen confidence and cooperation to help prevent crime and reduce the fear of crime.

community service. A form of judicial sanction in which the offender is ordered to perform a number of hours of work in the community as a part of the sentence. Reparation to society is often a prime consideration.

comparative criminology. The study of crime in two or more cultures in an effort to gain broader information and data for theory construction and crime-control modeling.

complaintless crime. Also termed "victimless crimes." Crimes that typically have a "willing victim" such as gambling, drug use and addiction, or prostitution, in which no one complains to the authorities about the crime.

Comstock, Anthony (1844-1915). An American moral crusader who secured strict New York state and federal legislation against obscene matter. He also organized the New York Society for the Suppression of Vice.

concentric-zone method. (Also referred to as ecological zones). A model of metropolitan areas that identifies concentric rings that have distinctive characteristics (*See*: Chicago School).

concurrent sentence. Sentences to incarceration on two or more counts or in separate cases in which the court orders that they be served simultaneously. For example, a defendant receives two five-year terms upon being convicted on two counts of robbery. Because the sentences are ordered to run concurrently, the person will serve a total of five years before release (*See*: consecutive sentence).

conditioning. The process of developing a desired behavior pattern through a series of repeated experiences. Generally of two types: first, classical or conditional learning is associated with the work of Ivan Pavlov and takes place when a reflex action comes to be associated with a stimulus that does not usually invokes it. In Pavlov's experiments, a bell rung after each feeding came to be associated with food and caused (after bell ringing) the subject dogs to salivate, even when food was no longer present; with operant or instrumental conditioning, behavior is maintained or modified by the consequences which follow. A reward or reinforcement immediately following the behavior will increase the probability that the behavior will continue or be repeated. If the consequence is undesirable or punishing then the probability of the behavior continuing is diminished. The consequence must be sufficiently strong to elicit the desired response (*See*: classical and operant conditioning).

Condorcet, Marquis de (1743-1794). A French philosopher who felt that mankind would eventually progress to ultimate perfection in enlightenment and virtue and would then have no need for police. Because that state had not yet been reached, however, he believed that laws should be centered around the good citizen. His concept of prison was one of the first models to include rehabilitation.

concordance rate. A measure of the similarity of criminal behavior that is used in studies of twins.

conduct norms. Norms that regulate the daily lives of people and that reflect the attitudes of the groups to which they belong. They have been classified into three types: folkways, mores, and laws.

conflict, class. In Marx's theory of social classes, conflict between two major classes—the bourgeoisie (the haves) and the exploited proletariat (the have nots) - is inevitable. This conflict passes through a number of stages: individual disputes; sporadic demonstrations on the basis of recognized common interests; organized economic struggle; organized political struggle; and finally revolution, which leads to a temporary dictatorship of the proletariat and the development of a socialist, classless society.

conflict model. A theory that views law as emerging from conflict between interest groups with differing degrees of power. Those who are rich and powerful will use their influence to protect their own interests usually at the expense of the less powerful. Contrast to the consensus model, which assumes agreement in the formulation of criminal law.

conflict perspective. An analytical perspective regarding social organization that asserts that conflict is a fundamental aspect of social life and will never be resolved.

conflict, social. The study of social conflict is an interdisciplinary enterprise, involving social scientists. Some view this type of conflict as dysfunctional - a manifestation of individual aggression triggered by frustration, or arising from unfavorable perceptions that individuals or groups have of one another. Other researchers feel that group competition serves a useful function by fostering in-group solidarity and pride in the accomplishments of one's own group, which necessitates unfavorable attitudes and images of other groups.

conflict subculture. A delinquent subculture oriented toward violence, identity, territory and in some cases, economics. The subculture often fights rival gangs. It arises in unstable neighborhoods lacking mature adult models for conventional behavior.

conflict theory. An attempt to analyze its causes and consequences and eventually to speculate about its resolution or regulation. Generalizations of human conflict have a long and rich history in philosophy and the social and behavioral sciences. Basically, conflict occurs when, instead of harmony, equilibrium, order, or consensus within or between persons, there is discontent, disagreement, struggle, or open fighting.

Social conflict is open struggle over either values and meanings or resources (property, income and power), or both. It occurs *within* as well as *between* all types and sizes of groups (clans, tribes, families, cities, nation-states, and the like).

Conflict theorizing is at least as old as conflict itself, but its orientation shifted radically with the writings of Karl Marx. Chinese, Greek, Arabian, Italian, and French theorists all speculated about such large-scale social conflicts as war and revolution before Marx. The British—Thomas Hobbes, David Hume, Adam Smith, Robert Malthus, and Charles Darwin—added a materialistic or scientific basis to the study of conflict. Marx viewed it in terms of the historical group struggles (between social classes) over property and production. Conflict theory since Marx has generally been in some way a reaction to his statements.

Other theories of social conflict are linked with values and ideology (Social Darwinism and Marxism are examples). Recent theory concerns the causes and outcomes of revolutionary conflict in the Third World and the relative absence of class conflict in contemporary capitalist societies (See: Dahrendorf, Ralf).

conflict theory of stratification. An explanation of the rise and maintenance of social inequality. According to the theory, social inequality is based upon a constant struggle among individuals and groups within that society over scarce resources, privileges, and rewards. This explanation is in stark contrast to functionalist theories, which see inequality as a necessary prerequisite of every society, based on a shared value system, and arising out of a society's need for coordination and cohesion.

Based more on Max Weber's concept of authority than on Karl Marx's views of class conflict, the most influential contemporary conflict theory of stratification is that of Ralf Dahrendorf. He views society as a network of "imperatively coordinated associations." These refer to a range of units from the state to business enterprises to trade unions. What these theories have in common is that they are characterized by "dominance relations," hierarchies of authority in which some members exert authority over others. Those possessing authority form a "quasi-group with latent interest," as do those lacking authority. Once a set of technical, political, and social conditions are met, these quasi-groups are transformed into groups with manifest interests, and social conflict over preservation or change in the status quo may begin.

While the logic of Dahrendorf's theory owes much to Marx, he sees the origins of both social inequality and social conflict in the authority differences that characterize every human organization. Therefore, unlike Marx, he sees no escape from either of these conditions, regardless of the form of economic organization adopted by a society.

conformity. The adaptation of an individual's behavior to society's patterns, norms, or standards. Compliance is the act of complying to rules or standards of behavior.

conjugal visits. A prison visitation program that permits sexual relations between prescribed members in a correctional setting. Generally, such overnight or weekend visits are limited to the inmates' legal spouses.

consecutive sentences. Sentences to incarceration on two or more counts or in separate cases where the court orders that they be served one after the other (*See*: concurrent sentence).

conservative criminology. A principle associated with Beccaria and Bentham. This approach is based on the pleasure-pain or hedonistic calculus theories holding that individuals know right from wrong, are capable of making free-will choices and must assume the responsibilities and consequences for their actions. This theory holds that the severity of punishment will serve as a deterrent to criminal conduct. Focus on deterrence, incapacitation, and retribution as crime control strategies. Also supports determinate sentencing, mandatory minimum sentences and the death penalty. Contemporary conservative criminologists include James Q. Wilson, Andrew Von Hirsch, and Ernest Van Den Haag (*See*: liberal and radical criminology).

consensus model. An analytical perspective regarding social organizations, which suggests that the majority of members of society agree as to what is right and what is wrong, and that the various elements of society work in unison toward a common and shared vision of the "greater good." According to this model, most people in society are in agreement with the prohibitions contained in the criminal law.

constitutional theories. Those criminological theories that tend to explain criminality by reference to offenders' body types, inheritance, genetics, or external observable physical characteristics (*See*: constitutional types; biological theories; somatotyping; Ernst Kretschmer; William H. Sheldon).

constitutional types. The classification of different types of human bodies, and the general theory that there exists a relationship between body types and personality and behavior traits. Ernest Kretschmer devised the first such theory in the 19th century, but the foremost system is that of William H. Sheldon, who identified three major types of physique: *endomorphy*, characterized by a round, fat, flabby appearance; *mesomorphy,* athletic and muscular; and *ectomorphy*, frail and thin. Though psychologists have not accepted the alleged relationship that these types have to behavior and personality, Sheldon's system does provide a convenient method of measuring and classifying body types (*See*: constitutional types; biological theories; somatotyping; Ernst Kretschmer; and William H. Sheldon).

constitutive criminology. The process by which human beings create an ideology of crime that sustains the notion of crime as a concrete reality.

containment. Accepted as those aspects of the social bond which act to prevent individuals from committing crimes and that keep them from engaging in deviant behavior. *Inner containment* refers to one's own control mechanisms such as moral values, self-esteem, and ability to defer gratification. *Outer containment* represents controls exerted by others, usually authority figures, such as parents, school officials and the police.

contingency. A factor that determines movement from one criminal role to another, or from one crime to another.

control theory. An concept of delinquency and crime that postulates that criminal and delinquent acts occur when the bonds that tie people to the law-abiding society are weakened. These bonds include attachment to others, commitment to conventional lines of action, involvement in conventional activity, and the belief in the laws and sanctions governing forbidden behavior.

convict subculture. The culture within the prison that is considered distinct from the outside society. The subculture within the prison is believed to have its own set of values, attitudes, and behaviors.

conviction. A determination or finding of guilt be it through a plea, a jury verdict, court verdict, or *nolo contendere.*

Cooley, Charles Horton (1875-1940). He was a sociologist who developed the concept of primary and secondary groups. Primary groups are face-to-face groups with whom we have close interactions. Secondary groups might be baseball or football teams or college fraternities or sororities. He developed the concept of the "looking-glass self." This view consisted of (1) our impressions of how others view us, (2) our interpretations of these impressions as either good or bad, and (3) our persistence or change in the behaviors eliciting the approval or disapproval of others.

corporal punishment. Pain inflicted on the body for the purpose of deterrence and retribution. Historically, conducted in public view to enhance the general deterrence effect. Punishments included flogging, branding, amputation and other painful acts.

corporate crime. A crime attributed to a corporation, but perpetrated by or on the authority of an officer or high managerial agent.

correctional psychology. A subset of forensic psychology concerned with the diagnosis and classification of offenders, the treatment of correctional populations, and the rehabilitation of inmates and other law violators.

corrections. The third component and final stage in the criminal justice system, which is responsible for the custody and control of the convicted offender after sentencing. The correctional system is made up of two components: institutional and community corrections. Institutional corrections involves those agencies and institutions responsible for maintaining physical custody of an offender and include juvenile hall, camps, and prisons. Community corrections comprises all correctional activity that takes place outside of an institution and includes probation, parole, electronic monitoring, halfway houses, therapeutic communities, and many other programs and agencies that exist outside of the prison walls.

cortical arousal. Activation of the cerebral cortex, a structure of the brain, which is responsible for higher intellectual functioning, information processing, and decision making.

court of last resort. The last and final step in the criminal appeals process is the U.S. Supreme Court. There is no further appeal of a U.S. Supreme Court decision.

crime. An act or omission in violation of law that either commands or forbids it to be done as generally defined in the penal or criminal code of a state or the federal government.

crime, causes of. The two broad categories of crime causation are considered to be classical and positivistic explanations. Classical theorists consider people to possess free will and to be rational beings while positivist (determinists) seek to discover the causes of criminality in biological, economic, sociological and psychological factors.

Explanations regarding agents or forces that determine or create violations of the law abound. The causes of crime have never been satisfactorily isolated. When used to explain the incidence of crime in general or of certain classes of crimes, the imputed causes are more likely to describe factors of greater or lesser risk for individuals of coming into contact with the criminal justice system. When used to explain the behavior of a single individual, causes represent attempts to factor individual cases by ordinary qualitative analysis or clinical diagnosis. The quest for causes of crime or of criminal behavior has been fraught with the difficulty of isolating the differential impact of situational factors on varying mental, environmental, and physical constitutions. It has also been hampered by the difficulty of demonstrating that a particular combination of factors applies to delinquents rather than to non- delinquents, or to delinquent behavior rather than to non-delinquent behavior.

crime-control model. A perspective on the criminal justice process proposing that the most important function of criminal justice is the repression of crime. The book, *The Limits of the Criminal Sanction*, by Herbert L. Packer in 1975, fully develops this concept, contrasting it with the due process model. The crime control model is central to Packer's adversarial or conflict theory, in which the goal of crime control is the quick and efficient processing of those who violate the law. (*See*: due process model).

crime, etiology of causation. The systematic study of the causes of criminal behavior (*See*: crime, causes of).

crime index. A set of numbers indicating the volume, fluctuation, and distribution of crimes reported to local law enforcement agencies, for the United States as a whole and for its geographical subdivisions, based on counts of reported occurrences of the FBI's annual *Uniform Crime Report's* (UCR) index crimes. These index crimes are murder and nonnegligent manslaughter, forcible rape, robbery, aggravated assault, burglary, larceny, theft, motor vehicle theft, and arson. All UCR Part 1 offenses except negligent (involuntary) manslaughter are index crimes. Negligent manslaughter is the only Part 1 offense lacking the feature of specific criminal intent. (*See:* crime rate).

crime, multiple causes of. As opposed to the concept of a single cause of crime, these explain multiple causes and fall into the category of what is referred to as integrated "theories." They include approaches such as congenital predisposition, mental retardation, or poverty. The multiple-causes approach posits several or many factors operating cumulatively to produce crime.

crime partner. The reference to an associate or accomplice in a crime or series of crimes.

crime rates. In national *Uniform Crime Report's* , published annually by the FBI, the crime rate is the number of crime index offenses known to police, per 100,000 population. In some state-level publications, crime rates are based on a different population unit, typically 1,000 persons. (*See:* crime index).

crimes of accommodation. Individual street crimes that, unlike crimes of resistance, do not represent "political" acts in response to social and economic exploitation and inequality but rather victimize, primarily, other working class and disadvantaged persons.

crimes of resistance. Violent and property street crimes involved in situations such as riots and revolts that have an explicitly political character, in response to perceived social and economic exploitation and inequalities.

criminal. Broadly, a person who has committed a crime; but legally and statistically, only a person who has been convicted of a crime. The attempt to limit the concept of "criminal" to persons who have committed serious crimes or those whose motives are distinctly evil involves value judgments that have no scientific basis and is therefore at odds with modern criminal justice practices.

criminal anthropology. A criminological theory of Cesare Lombroso, postulating that there are discernible and identifiable criminal types (*See*: born criminal; atavistic criminal).

criminal attempts. An act or omission constituting an overt act (a substantial step) in a course of conduct planned to culminate in the commission of a crime.

criminal behavior. A term sometimes synonymous with crime or violations of criminal code, but general usage places the emphasis on the behavior itself, whether or not it is known to authorities. The term can embrace violations of all codes or rules: those of family, church, school, labor unions, and other associations. What makes behavior legally criminal is that it involves offenses against codes that are reportable to governmental or state authorities and have attached sanctions.

criminal biology. The scientific study of the relation of hereditary (inherited) physical traits to criminal character, that is, to innate tendencies to commit crime in general or crimes of any particular type. It may also include the study of inherited personality traits and low IQ, which may predispose an individual toward criminal behavior.

criminal, born. A concept according to which certain persons are biologically so constituted that they must of necessity be criminals; a hereditary criminal. The study of the "born criminal" is associated with the work of Cesare Lombroso, the "father of criminology." While Lombroso's work has since been discredited, he has the distinction of being the first to use the scientific method to study criminal behavior. Raffaele Garofalo shared Lombroso's belief that certain physical traits lead to criminality.

criminal careers. A concept that describes the onset of criminal activity, the types and amount of crime committed, and the termination of such activity.

criminal culture. An integrated set of overt practices and ideas characteristic of a group of people and in conflict with the criminal law. A particular criminal act may be supported by, and be a part of, the criminal culture, which would include similar acts by other members of the group. In contrast, embezzlement and murder are often committed without the support of any criminal culture (*See*: subculture theory).

criminal, endogenic. A term used by European criminologists to describe a type of offenders whose criminality is determined mainly by hereditary and constitutional (both physical and mental) factors.

criminal, exogenic. A term used by European criminologists to designate a type of offender whose behavior is caused primarily by situational or environmental factors.

criminalistics. The science of crime detection using classical scientific methodology.

criminal justice. In the strictest sense, the criminal (penal) law, the law of criminal procedure, and that array of procedures and activities having to do with the enforcement of this body of law. The federal Crime Control Act of 1973 defined the term as part of a longer phrase: "Law enforcement and criminal justice means any activity pertaining to crime prevention, control, or reduction or the enforcement of the criminal law, including, but not limited to, police efforts to prevent, control, or reduce crime or to apprehend criminals, activities of courts having criminal jurisdiction and related agencies (including prosecutorial and defender services), activities of corrections, probation, or parole authorities, and programs relating to the prevention, control, or reduction of juvenile delinquency or narcotic addiction."

criminal justice process. The various stages from arrest to termination of official jurisdiction (*See:* criminal justice; criminal justice system).

criminal justice system. Composed of the various agencies of "justice," to protect society. The term specifically refers to the activities of police, courts, probation, and corrections, whose goal it is to apprehend, convict, punish, and rehabilitate law violators.

criminal justice wedding cake. The concept of the wedding cake was developed by Lawrence Friedman and Robert V. Percival in *The Roots of Justice*. Additional support, based on contemporary evidence, is found in Michael and Don Gottfredson's *Decision Making in Criminal Justice*. The wedding cake model emphasizes the differences in the response to different kinds of criminal cases. There are great differences *among* each of the four layers, but fairly consistent patterns within each layer. The small top layer consists of those celebrated cases receiving wide media coverage. Celebrated cases give the public a distorted view of the criminal justice system and process. The second and third layers are felony cases divided by the nature and seriousness of the offense(s). The fourth layer, generally out of sight, comprises all the misdemeanors.

criminaloids. A term originating with Cesare Lombroso to describe occasional criminals who were pulled into criminality primarily by environmental influences.

criminal man. The conception of the criminal as an individual possessing distinctive physical or psychical characteristics (*See*: born criminal).

criminal maturation. The development of a criminal in the established techniques, attitudes, and ideology of criminal behavior. The phrase assumes that such development follows a standard pattern analogous to physiological development with advancing age.

criminal, pathological. The term "pathological" means that the behavior or criminality is indicative of a disease. The origins of the "disease" will be located in social, biological, or mental factors depending on the discipline, i.e., social, biological, or psychological determinism/positivism. It is a term used by the "medical model" which seeks to diagnose and treat criminal behavior as symptomatic of a social disease. It is also an attempt to make a prognosis once a treatment plan is established. The term is associated with the positivistic school of thought.

criminal sanction. The penalties attached to violation and conviction of the criminal law.

criminal tendencies. A disposition or inclination to be involved in criminal behavior. Origins of criminal tendencies vary considerably depending on the philosophical perspective (i.e. biological, sociological, psychological).

criminal typologies. This subarea of criminology involves the study of certain "types" of crimes and their patterns. Crime "types" include violent crime, theft, public disorder crimes, and white collar crime. There is considerable research which attempts to understand the origins of specific crimes.

criminogenesis. All those factors that give birth to, give rise to, cause, or generate crime.

criminologist. A generic term to describe one who is trained or educated in the field of criminology. Also, one who studies crime, criminals, and criminal behavior. One who attempts to determine the causes of crime.

criminology. The study of crime causation and crime theory. Criminology had its origins in the Enlightenment of the 18th century, where such men as Cesare Beccaria and Jeremy Bentham explored ways of making criminal law a more just and humane state instrument. The 19th century saw the rise of the positivist school, which stressed the need for a scientific understanding of the causes of crime and its control. In the United States in the early 1900s, criminology was largely in the domain of the social sciences, particularly sociology. The mid-1900s saw criminology emerging into a separate and distinct field of study.

In the study of crime, two major trends can be discerned. First, in the search for the causes of criminal behavior, attention has shifted from individual characteristics to aspects of the social environment in which the individual functions. Second, in attempting to curb criminal behavior, the emphasis shifted from punishment and deterrence to efforts at rehabilitation and back again to punishment and the imprisonment of offenders. However, criminology as an evolving and emerging science still lacks a proven theory of the causes of crime (other than opportunity), and different methods of preventing crime do not rest on precise scientific evidence. In recent years increasing attention has been directed toward the structure and function of criminal law.

crisis intervention. The forestalling of a usually undesirable crucial and significant event or a decisive and radical change in a person's life. The definition of "crisis" will vary among individuals and cultures, but traditionally only certain roles in society were seen as oriented toward bringing relief to the stress of a particular event, such as the death of a loved one. Recently, however, groups have formed clinics and telephone answering services in attempts to relieve strain and give counsel in many less specific situations. Hotlines, such as suicide prevention, spousal abuse and rape crisis centers, provide callers with supportive and referral options.

Crofton, Sir Walter (1815-1897). He was director of the Irish prison system in 1846. Crofton improved upon the ticket-of-leave system established by Alexander Maconochie by including provisions for revocation of the ticket-of-leave if conditions were violated. He also included provisions for supervision of released inmates by police officials. (*See* Maconochie; progressive system).

cruel and unusual punishment. Punishment that is so excessive or out of proportion to the magnitude of the crime that it is violation of the Eighth Amendment to the Constitution of the United States. The federal courts have frequently found state prison systems to be in violation of the 8th amendment due to gross overcrowding and associated conditions. In 1980, the U.S. Supreme Court in the case of *Estelle vs. Ruiz*, found the entire Texas prison system in violation of the Eighth Amendment.

After the resumption of the death penalty in 1976, U.S. Supreme Court justices Thurgood Marshal and William Brennan objected to this sanction on the grounds that capital punishment was cruel and unusual punishment. From 1976 to their retirement in the 1990s, they voiced dissent in over 2,500 cases.

cultural patterns or universal patterns. Accepted patterns that are supposed to be followed.

culture. The sum total of ways of living built up by a group of human beings and transmitted from one generation to another; the behaviors and beliefs characteristic of a particular social, ethnic, or age group (See: subcultural theories)

culture deviance theory. A branch of social structure that combines the concepts of social disorganization and strain theories to describe how individuals in depressed or disadvantaged neighborhoods react to their conditions of deprivation. Because their lives are filled with stress, financial hardship, and material deprivation, people in the lower-class develop a distinct "subculture" with its own set of rules, values, and behaviors. Perhaps the best known cultural deviance theory is that of Walter Miller, who in 1958 wrote *Lower Class Culture as a Generating Milieu of Gang Delinquency*. In his study, Miller described the distinct value system of lower-class culture. Adherence to what Miller termed "focal concerns" such as trouble, toughness, smartness, excitement, fate, and autonomy often lead to confrontations with the police because they clash with middle-class standards. Miller differs from Cohen in that Miller does not believe that lower-class values necessarily represent a rebellion against middle-class values. Instead, these values have developed as a result of conditions present in lower-class culture.

Cultural deviance theory posits that crime results from cultural values which permit, or even demand, behavior in violation of the law (*See*: subcultural theory).

cultural transmission. In Social Structure Theory the belief that the values, attitudes, and behavior are passed on from one generation to the next. Usually refers to lower-class subculture.

culture conflict. Described by Thorsten Sellin as a condition that results when the demands and expectations of a particular subculture come into conflict with variously socialized groups over what is acceptable or proper behavior (*See*: subcultural and cultural deviance theory).

culture of poverty. A way of life characterized by helplessness, cynicism, present-orientation, lack of community ties, physical inclination, a lack of political awareness or action, and mistrust of authority as represented by schools, police and other vested power. This concept was described by Oscar Lewis in 1966 and by Edward C. Banfield in *The Unheavenly City* and *The Unheavenly City Revisited.*

cycloid. A term coined by Ernst Kretschmer to describe a particular relationship between body build and personality type. The cycloid personality, which was associated with a heavy-set, soft type of body, was said to vacillate between normality and abnormality.

D

D.A.R.E. One of the most popular recent antidrug education programs, the Drug Awareness Resistance Education, was created by the Los Angeles Police Department in 1983 and subsequently adopted in many other jurisdictions across the nation.

D.A.R.E. uses an affective education approach with a strong emphasis on values clarification, "providing the skills for recognizing and resisting social pressures to experiment with tobacco, alcohol, and drugs," and "developing skills in risk assessment and decision making." The program consists of seventeen 45- to 60-minute sessions for fifth and sixth grade students, taught by sworn police officers. Nationally, five million students were exposed to D.A.R.E. training in 1991.

Dahrendorf, Ralf. He was a conflict theorist who asserted that society is organized into imperatively coordinated associations and divided into two distinct groups: one group possesses authority and uses it for social domination; the other group lacks authority and is dominated. He authored *Class and Conflict in Industrial Society* (1959). He also posited that social conflict is pervasive and persistent, that coercion is the controlling element in social organization, and that each individual is an element potentially possessing the power to change society, and that every society is capable of being changed.

Darwin, Charles Robert (1809-1882). British scientist and naturalist. His major work was *The Origin of the Species* (1859). His evolutionary theories changed the course of thinking in almost every scientific discipline. Perhaps the most significant was his principle of natural selection: those organisms survive that are best suited to their environment and its requirements for living. Darwin also contended that there was continuity of mind and body between human and all other species.

data. Collected facts, observations, and other pertinent information from which conclusions can be drawn.

day fines. An intermediate sanction whereby the court considers a defendant's daily income as a method to implement fairness in sentencing because a wealthy offender will be less impacted by the same fine imposed on someone who is poor.

day-reporting centers. An intermediate sanction whereby an offender is required to report to a facility during the daytime hours and then allowed to go home in the evening. Frequently used for probation and parole violators as an alternative to incarceration.

deconstructionist theories. These are emerging approaches that challenge existing criminological perspectives to disprove them, and work toward replacing them with concepts more applicable to the post-modern era. One radical criminology theory suggests that common terms are as value laden as societal rules and regulations. As such they reflect the inequities of the social structure, which are directly influenced by capitalism.

decriminalization. A reduction in the severity of penalties. For example, several jurisdictions have reduced the penalty for possession of less than one ounce of marijuana an infraction rather than a misdemeanor. A person is cited instead of arrested.

defendant. The person charged with a crime in a legal proceeding; the accused. Also used in civil proceedings to identify the respondent.

defense mechanism. An attempt by an individual to use cognitive strategies to cope with unpleasant realities and fear, such as conflict, frustration, shame, and anger. Defense mechanisms were first identified by Freud in 1894. He defined them as a function of the ego, which mediates between the primitive impulses of the id and the moral demands of the superego. When these two forces come into conflict, there is a sudden increase in tension. The ego will use a variety of techniques to reduce the tension —and it was these Freud called defense mechanisms. Defense mechanisms, or coping strategies, include denial of reality, day dreaming, rationalization, projection, repression, regression and reaction formation.

defensible space. Considered to be the range of mechanisms that combine to bring an environment under the control of its residents.

defounding. The process of statistically lowering unsolved felonies to misdemeanors.

deindividuation. A loss of self-awareness during which one behaves with little or no reference to personal internal values or standards of conduct. Deindividuated states are extremely pleasurable to experience, in that one feels free to act on impulse and without regard to consequences. They can also be extremely dangerous, in that they can result in violent antisocial behavior.

deinstitutionalization. A public policy that began in the 1970s to move confined mental patients out of secure facilities into the community. Also applied to certain types of offenders in the juvenile and adult justice system. In criminal justice, deinstitutionalization is best known for removing juvenile status offenders from locked facilities.

delinquency. Many jurisdictions define delinquency as "any act which, if committed by an adult, would be a crime." However, status offenses are violations of juvenile or under age-directed laws such as curfew, consumption of alcoholic beverages, truancy, tobacco and the like. Status offenses and violations of criminal codes committed by juveniles can be considered acts of delinquency.

Delinquency statutes were enacted at the turn of the century, beginning with the Illinois Juvenile Court Act of 1899, in an attempt to shield young offenders from the stigmatizing effect of being treated as criminals. An unintended consequence of this reform has been to "criminalize" the uninhibited youth who does not conform as expected. The scope and vagueness of delinquency laws were severely criticized as early as 1925, when the National Probation Association first drafted the Standard Juvenile Court Act. This act and subsequent recommendations to limit the "inflated" scope of delinquency resulted in legislation is some states to separate law-violating behavior from non-law-violating misbehavior. In New York and several other states a new classification arose for persons in this latter category; they were identified as "persons in need of supervision." Further strictures on the legal processing of minors were set forth in the Supreme Court decision *In re Gault* in 1967, which was the first such decision extending some of the guarantees of the Constitution to minors.

A delinquent is a minor who has been adjudicated by the juvenile court. Agencies of social control, such as schools, welfare organizations, parents, and the police, may initiate petitions to the court, which then decide whether or not the youth is delinquent. Each such agency has its own concept of what constitutes delinquent conduct.

Numerous explanation have been postulated regarding the cause(s) of juvenile delinquency.

Biological approaches rely on the idea that because of defects in heredity, the youth suffers from brain pathology or that due to glandular or chromosomal imbalance or a certain body structure, he or she has a temperament prone to delinquent behavior.

Psychological approaches seek explanations of delinquency in personality maladjustment; that is, the delinquent misbehaves in response to some kind of psychological pathology. Those who use such explanations vary in their emphases, depending on whether the orientation is that of psychoanalysis, psychiatry, or clinical psychology.

Sociological or Criminological approaches seek to explain delinquency by describing conditions in the social structure, such as poverty or "blocked opportunity"; the delinquent subculture in which the patterns are learned; and, more recently, the impact on the individual's process of becoming delinquent as a consequence of the impact on his or her self-concept of the label imposed by social-control agents.

demography. The statistical study of population size, composition, distribution and patterns of change.

demonology. The belief that people who violate the law are possessed by evil spirits and that their criminality can be corrected only by the removal of those spirits.

dependent personality disorder. Traits include submissive and clinging behavior. The unhealthy exaggeration of basic needs which must be satisfied by other people, particularly the need for mothering, love, affection, shelter, protection, security, physical care, food and warmth. Persons suffering from this disorder fail to develop traits of self-confidence, decisiveness, and self-reliance.

deprivation model. Holds that the values, attitudes, and behaviors found in the prison subculture results from the adaptation to the pains (deprivations) of imprisonment (*See*: importation model).

desert-based sentences. Sentences that consider the offender's prior record and seriousness nature of the offense rather than personal characteristics (*See*: just deserts).

determinate sentences. Also called fixed sentences. Some determinate sentencing structures, like those in California allow for a low-, mid-, and high-range sentence. The court is obligated to impose, a mid-range sentence unless there are mitigating or aggravating factors present. Mitigating factors might result in a low-end sentence, while aggravating factors might result in a sentence at the high range. The major advantages of these sentences is that discretion and uncertainty are removed and inmates know exactly when they will be released (See: indeterminate sentences)

deterrence strategy. A conservative crime-control approach to diminish motivation for crime by increasing the certainty and severity of sanctions.

deterrence theories. Deterrence is a theory suggesting that swift and sure punishment will discourage others from similar illegal acts.

general. Criminal sanctions provided to deter the community or society at-large from committing criminal acts.

specific. The administration of punishment on the offender in the hope that he or she will refrain from further crime in order to avoid repetition of the punishment. The use of capital punishment, for example, is classified as a specific deterrent as the offender will never commit another crime.

deviance. Behavior that violates social norms. Deviant behavior may not always be a crime, and certain crimes may not represent deviant behavior.

Devil's Island. For nearly a century, from 1852 to 1947, French convicts were sent to this penal colony located off the coast of French Guiana (*See*: transportation).

Dickens, Charles (1812-1870). One of the world's greatest novelists, this English writer used his books as a method of exposing abuses in all areas of society. Through such classics as *Great Expectations* and *Oliver Twist*, Dickens was responsible for enlisting public support against abuses in prisons, schools, hospitals, and the government. His criticism of society was largely moral, for he believed that the abuses were caused by cruelty, selfishness, and hardness of heart.

Diderot, Denis (1713-1784). The French encyclopedist, novelist, dramatist, art critic, and philosopher who attacked the orthodoxy of his time. He revolted against the unquestioning acceptance of tradition and authority and, in many of his works, he heavily criticized the chaos and corruption in political institutions as well as the superstition and cruelty that pervaded penal practices.

differential assocation reinforcement. A theory of criminality based on the incorporation of psychological learning theory and differential association with social learning theory. Criminal behavior, the theory suggests, is learned through associations and is continued or discontinued as a result of positive or negative reinforcements.

differential association theory. Formulated by Edwin Sutherland and suggested, contrary to beliefs of the 1930s, that criminal behavior did not result from either hereditary factors or the simple opportunity to commit crime. Opportunity factors, Sutherland asserted, were necessary but not sufficient. There had to be opportunity, but because not all persons would make use of this opportunity to commit a deviant act, the presence of opportunity could not, in itself, explain crime. In Sutherland's example, when there was no liquor available in Germany during World War I, there were no arrests for intoxication; without opportunity, no deviance occurred. But even when opportunity is present, crime may or may not occur; when liquor became available, only some Germans were arrested for intoxication. Thus, another explanation is necessary.

Sutherland observed that criminal behavior requires specialized learning. This learning involves both abilities (specific techniques, such as opening locks and avoiding alarms), and also inclinations. These inclinations regard illegal behavior as a favorable activity. Individuals acquire both abilities and inclinations in groups. The principle of differential association is that an individual will tend to commit criminal activity when his or her associations with groups that teach criminal abilities and favor criminal inclinations are more important that those associations with noncriminal groups. The importance of an association with a group was based on the *frequency* of that association (how often the individual was in the group), the *duration* of association (how long in the group), and the *intensity* of association or involvement.

Differential association theory was among the first attempts to explain a form of behavior in exclusively social terms. In Sutherland's work, criminal behavior was no longer regarded to be a result of psychological, physiological, or geographical factors but was explained through the experience of the criminal in society: his or her group associations. Sutherland also suggested that his theory worked equally well for what he called "white collar" crime, because among businessmen there could also be a group attitude favorable to certain illegalities, such as tax fraud, violations of safety codes, or embezzlement. Thus, the types of crime committed will result more from the nature of the criminal's group involvements that from something about the criminal as an individual.

A version of Differential Association Theory developed by Daniel Glaser in his book *Crime in Our Changing Society* (1978), wherein he combines social learning concepts with his belief that expectations control behavior. Glaser defines the origins expectations as pro- and anti-criminal social bonds, differential learning, and perceived opportunities. The major element is that people become involved in criminality with the "anticipated" gains outweighing the potential punishment.

At its highest level of generality, the theory of differential association becomes a theory of social process, suggesting that the more groups favoring illegality there are within a society, the more disorganized that society has become. Thus, the type of crime committed will result form the nature of the actor's group association than from psychological or individual factors.

differential opportunity theory. A theory explaining delinquent and criminal behavior, which emphasizes the access or lack of access people have to both legal and illegal ways of meeting their individual goals. A major conclusion of differential opportunity theory is that access to illegitimate opportunities or criminal remedies may also be limited or closed.

differential social organization. The initial rendition of differential association theory. Edwin Sutherland used the concepts of differential social organization and culture conflict to provide an explanation of why crime rates vary from group to group. Sutherland asserted that conflict is widespread and is produced by a disorganized society. This conflict and disorganization results in a number of distinct groups with their own values. Inevitably, according to Sutherland, some of these groups will clash with existing laws, resulting in criminality.

dipsomania. Alcoholism. A mental disorder manifested by an uncontrollable desire for intoxicating drink; an irresistible impulse to indulge in intoxication, either by alcohol or other drugs.

discretion. The freedom to use one's own judgment in reaching a decision. Criminal justice personnel tend to have substantial discretion. A major criticism of too much discretion is that it leads to disparity.

displacement. The process by which an emotion originally attracted to a particular person, object, or situation is transferred to something else. The unacceptable feelings are usually transferred from an object that is of central importance in the person's life to an external object that is relatively harmless. A child who is angry with a parent(s) may kick a animal or an inanimate object as a substitute for striking its' parent(s). They generally remain unaware of where the hostility was originally focused.

disposition. The term is used in juvenile court to refer to outcome or sentencing after adjudication or guilt has been established.

disturbing the peace. The unlawful interruption of the peace, quiet, or order of a community, including offenses called "disorderly conduct," "vagrancy," "loitering," "unlawful assembly," and "riot."

diversion. An alternative to processing through the criminal justice system. In diversion cases, processing is halted or suspended pending the completion of an educational or treatment program. When the offender completes the program, the completion certificate is provided to the court, which then dismisses the charges. If the offender fails to complete the program, criminal proceedings may be reinstituted.

Dix, Dorothea Lynde (1802-1887). She devoted over half of her life to the reform of mental institutions in the United States and in Europe. In 1841, while teaching a Sunday school class at the East Cambridge Massachusetts House of Correction, she observed that the insane were imprisoned with criminals and treated as subhuman. Dix immediately began a two-year investigation of jails and alms houses in Massachusetts. Her efforts resulted in public response and having legislation enacted to reform the treatment of mental patients. The result was the founding of state asylums for treatment, rather an imprisoning mental patients.

Doe, Charles (1830-1896). He was appointed at the age of 29 as associate justice to the supreme court in New Hampshire. Doe served in that capacity from 1859 to 1874 and as chief justice from 1876 until his death. He is mainly remembered for substantial accomplishments in the field of evidence and procedure, as well as his work with Isaac Ray in formulating the New Hampshire Rules. Long before Supreme Court justice Benjamin Cardozo and legal scholar Roscoe Pound made their pleas for the integration of law and science, Doe had been the first judge to insist that law should collaborate with science, particularly in the field of criminal responsibility.

double jeopardy. Relates to the Fifth Amendment of the Constitution, which prohibits a person from being tried on the same charge a second time.

Draconian Code. The legal code designed by Dracon of Athens in the seventh century B.C. that made death the punishment for every crime.

dramaturgy (also dramaturgical perspective). A theoretical point of view that depicts human behavior as centered around the purposeful management of interpersonal impressions.

drive-reduction theory. The American experimental psychologist Clark Hill (1884-1952) proposed the principle that learning takes place only when a fundamental drive or need is reduced. For example, when an animal learns to avoid shock, its performance of the avoidance response reduces the fear of being shocked. This fear reduction strengthens the avoidance response. Drive-reduction theory has been proposed generally to account for learning that occurs when punishment is employed.

driving under the influence (DUI). Driving or operating any vehicle or common carrier while drunk or under the influence of liquor or drugs.

drift. According to David Matza, a state of limbo in which youths move in and out of delinquency and in which their lifestyles can embrace both conventional and deviant values.

drug abuse violations. These are offenses related to growing, manufacturing, making, possessing, using, selling, or distributing narcotic and dangerous nonnarcotic drugs. A distinction is made between possession and sale/manufacturing.

drug abuse surveys.
The National Household Survey, sponsored by the National Institute on Drug Abuse (NIDA), periodically col-

lects self-reported data on drug use from 4,000 to 6,000 households.

The National High School Senior Drug Abuse Survey is a self-reporting survey of 2,400 seniors from 130 public and private schools.

The Drug Abuse Warning Network (DAWN) reports drug-related deaths and drug-related visits to emergency rooms from over 700 hospitals in 21 metropolitan areas and from 87 medical examiners (or coroners) in 27 metropolitan areas.

The Drug Use Forecasting (DUF) program collects urine specimens and self-reported data on drug use from persons arrested in 24 cities.

drunkenness. Public intoxication by the voluntary use of alcoholic beverages other than driving under the influence.

dualistic fallacy. The supposition that a particular population has two mutually exclusive subclasses: for example, delinquents and nondelinquents.

due process model. A philosophy based on the assumption that an individual is presumed innocent until proven guilty and that individuals ought to be protected from arbitrary power of the state. (*See:* Crime control model).

due process. The guarantee that a person shall not be deprived of all the judicial rights to which he or she is legally entitled. What is required, however, is subject to interpretation by the court.

Dugdale, Richard (1841-1883). He authored *The Jukes: A Study in Crime, Pauperism, Disease and Heredity* (1877), advocating that heredity is responsible for the genetic transmission of criminal traits.

Durham rule. A defense of insanity, used in New Hampshire and elsewhere, which requires that criminal proceedings be suspended if it is determined that the offender committed the crime as a result of mental illness (*See:* M'Naghten rule).

Durkheim, Emile (1858-1917). French sociologist who held that religion and morality originate in the collective mind of society and used anthropology and statistics to support his theories. Durkheim had a strong influence on the disciplines of sociology and criminology. His study on suicide rates found that suicide was a function of social rather than psychological processes. He found that suicide rates varied from group to group, the common factor being a person's isolation from others. To the extent that a person possessed social bonds he or she was at a lower suicide risk. His eminence in the field of criminology rests upon his broad approach to antisocial behavior. In *The Rules of the Sociological Method* (1965), Durkheim claimed that a society without crime is impossible. Because a society must necessarily contain a diverse grouping of people, deviation and hence crime is inevitable. Durkheim, therefore, felt that crime was normal and in fact felt that a society without crime would be one of profound pathology. A society without crime would be pathological in that it represents a state of absolute conformity through such rigidity. Such a society would be closed to any social change and hence progress. Crime is simply the price a society pays in exchange for progress and change. In his *Rules of the Sociological Method*, Durkheim also developed the concept of anomie. This condition arises when the institutions of society break down and can no longer regulate the behaviors of its inhabitants.

E

early onset. Refers to the belief that chronic offenders or career criminals begin their crime early in life, and this criminality continues well into adulthood. The juvenile who commences delinquency early in adolescence will generally continue to commit crime as an adult.

ecological theory. Commonly termed the "Chicago School" of criminology; a type of sociological approach that emphasizes demographics and geographies and views the social disorganization which characterizes delinquency areas as a major cause of criminality and victimization (*See*: social structure theory; concentric zones).

ecology. The study of the distribution of people and their activities in time and space; used in the study of criminal and other kinds of deviant behavior in relationship to environmental circumstances in which the behavior occurs.

econometrics. A theory of crime developed largely by Gary S. Becker in his book *The Economics of Crime* (1968), which is similar to Classical Theory. Economic determinism holds that people conduct a form of cost-benefit analysis before deciding whether or not to commit an illegal act. Econometrics refers to the use of mathematical techniques to test and apply economic theories. The most widely cited econometric study is that of Isaac Ehrlich (*See*: Ehrlich's "Magic Bullet" theory).

ectomorph. A body type described as being a thin, wiry, and easily excitable person not prone to committing crimes.

ego. That part of the psyche that, according to psychoanalytic theory, governs rational behavior. The ego is a moderator between the superego and the id.

Ehrlich's "Magic Bullet" theory. Economist Dr. Isaac Ehrlich claimed in 1975 that each execution deterred seven or eight murders. The U.S. Supreme Court cited Ehrlich's evidence in its 1976 *Gregg* decision upholding the constitutionality of the death penalty. His research was based on the "rational choice theory" of human behavior. He stated "the propensity to perpetrate such crimes is influenced by the prospective gains and losses associated with their commission."

electroencephalogram (EEG). A machine used by doctors and hospitals to measure the electrical impulses of the brain. Used to determine if neurological anomalies are present. Biological positivists have conducted research to determine if violent offenders and or career criminals have abnormal brain waves.

embezzlement. The crime of withholding or withdrawing (conversion or misappropriation), without consent, funds entrusted to an agent (e.g., a bank teller or officer).

empathy. Relating to the position, thoughts, reaction or feelings of another person. Also, sympathy, compassion, and/ or understanding.

employment prison. A confinement facility for low-risk inmates. Prisoners work at jobs outside the prison during the day but return to prison after work. (*See*: work furlough)

Engels, Friedrich (1820-1895). He was an associate of Karl Marx and collaborated in the formulation of economic determinism and the conflict perspective and in writing of the *Communist Manifesto* (1848). He wrote *The Condition of the Working Class in England* in 1844. He was a

German social revolutionary and member of the Communist League who viewed society as a class struggle between those who own the means of production (bourgeoisie) and those who labor for them (proletariat). This class system produces conflict regarding profit and survival. He also posited that crime is a function of social demoralization and that workers become embroiled in a milieu of frustrations which lead to violence and crime. The capitalist system causes workers to become criminals despite their will to act in conventional and socially approved ways.

entrapment. A legal defense that asserts that the arresting party arranged the criminal action or planted the criminal idea.

environmental factors in crime causation. This generally refers to sociological determinism, which sees crime as a function of the social environment, be it Social Structural theory which focuses on how society is stratified and lacks opportunities, or Social Process theory, which emphasizes the learning of deviant behavior patterns in the process of socialization. Environmental factors in crime causation may also refer to a branch of biological determinism, which studies the impact of environmental chemicals and contaminants that influence behavior (*See*: social process and social structure theories).

epidemiological criminology. Investigation into how and why crime rates vary across classes of people or across time and space. For instance, crime rates vary with particular environmental conditions and geographic areas. Epidemiology entails the study of the incidence of crime under varied conditions, such as economic, social, or political. This field of inquiry also addresses the amount of victimization and the fear of crime in society.

episodic criminal. Generally referred to as situational offender; a person who commits a crime under extreme emotional stress, as the single exception to an otherwise lawful life; for example, an individual who kills in the heat of passion. This offender poses a problem for correctional officers because they are usually not in need of treatment and pose little or no risk of recidivism.

equal protection. A clause in the 14th Amendment of the U.S. Constitution that guarantees equal protection of the law to everyone, without regard to race, origin, economic class, age, gender, or religion.

equity. Natural, ethical justice. A system of justice developed and administered by the English court of chancery. Equity continues to exist in the United States, but due to the general abolition of the old dual system of courts, a sharp distinction is no longer made between actions of law and suits in equity. Common law was rigorously enforced by the law courts in England, with results that were often considered unjust. The only relief was petitions to the king, who tended to refer them to his chancellor. In time the petitions came to be addressed directly to the chancellor, and thus his authority to grant relief became institutionalized by the reign of Edward I (1272-1307). When the letter of the law was inadequate, an injured party looked to equity for relief.

Esquirol, Jean Etienne (1772-1840). A French psychiatrist and pupil of Philippe Pinel, Esquirol worked hard for the reform of mental institutions and for sympathetic treatment of the criminally insane. In his chief work, *Des Maladies Mentales*, he was one of the first people to emphasize the role of emotions as a source of mental disturbances.

ethnic cleansing. An organized purge of one group of people by another due to differing religious beliefs or ethnic backgrounds.

etiology of crime. The science of originating factors, as distinguished from final causes, of crime; the causes or reasons for crime; also, specific causes underlying criminal attitudes and behavior; the factors associated with but not necessarily causing crime. Certain types of criminals are closely related to particular kinds of social environment; others, to patterns of emotional development.

eugenics. The study of hereditary enhancement by genetic control.

euthenics. The branch of science that attempts to improve man by maintaining or improving the environment. This approach is contrasted with *eugenics*, the view that selective breeding is the way to improvement.

exchange theory. A general theory that treats human behavior as a process in which individuals supply one another with valued services, goods or benefits. In order for an exchange to continue, both parties must value the exchange. This theory has been applied most frequently to the analysis of power and differentiation in organizations, but it has also been used to analyze behavior in other social settings and relationships.

Differentiation in exchange relations occurs when the exchange is unequal. Power differences emerge when one person has control over resources valued by another. The disadvantaged party can reciprocate by rewarding the "supplier" with willing compliance. This reciprocity forms the basis of legitimate authority that is central to the functioning of organizations. The collective approval of the exercise of power establishes authority relations. Collective disapproval leads to opposition and conflict.

exclusionary rule. This relates to the Fourth Amendment to the Constitution: "The right of the people to be secure in their persons, houses, papers and effects, against unreasonable searches and seizures shall not be violated and no warrants shall issue, but upon probable cause." Examples of violations would be illegal searches, seizures, arrests and lineups.

ex parte. A hearing or examination in the presence of only one party in the case.

explanation. Refers to attempts to find an answer for the causes of crime. Criminological theories are an attempt to determine the etiology or the causes of crime and delinquency. There are various perspectives depending on the particular discipline. Therefore, we refer to (or combinations of) biological, psychological, sociological, environmental, and economic explanations.

expunge. To physically destroy court information, A case may be expunged or erased from the record by a plaintiff based on a court order. When expunged, it is as if the case never existed. The term expunge may also reflect legislated removal of an individual's record in certain offenses. In Massachusetts, for example, a person who is found to be in possession of marijuana as a first offense, if found guilty, may have a finding continued for six months at which time the case is brought forward and the record ordered expunged.

extroversion. According to Hans Eysenck, a dimension of the human personality. The term describes individuals who are sensation-seeking, dominant, and assertive, and therefore more prone to criminal behavior.

F

family therapy. Any form of group therapy in which interactions among family members, rather than the problems of a single family member, are the primary focus. Frequently, one family member does have clearly identifiable problems, but family therapy proceeds on the assumption that those problems are intimately related to problems of family dynamics. Generally, all the members of a nuclear family—parents and children—are involved. In the case of juvenile offenders, the court may mandate family therapy as a remedial part of the sanction(s). Of the variety of approaches to family therapy, two are most popular: (1) the *systems approach*, which explores the interrelated roles that family members play and the psychological functions those roles serve; and (2) the *communications* or *strategic approach*, which focuses on improving the ways in which family members communicate with one another and on fostering a family system that fulfills the needs of all family members.

fee system. A system, used in some areas, in which the county government pays a modest amount of money for each prisoner per day as an operating budget.

felony. A serious crime such as rape, homicide, or aggravated assault. Punishments typically range from more than one year confinement to death and the loss of many civil rights.

feminist theory. Attempts to address the ways in which socially structured categories of gender shape relations between men and women in the workplace and in organized family life. Scholars debate the extent to which other social relations affect, and are affected by, gender relations. A key issue is the extent to which gender can be analyzed in isolation from class and other factors.

Betty Friedan's book, *The Feminine Mystique* (1963), urged women to reevaluate their traditional roles and to demand opportunities equal to men's. Radical feminism, given its most comprehensive expression in Shulamith Firestone's 1970 book, *The Dialectic of Sex*, contends that women's burden in reproducing humankind is the basis for oppression by men. Firestone traces the ways in which biological inequality was perpetuated through the institutions of marriage and family.

Modern advancements in birth control, including abortion and safe childbirth techniques, offer the material means for women's freedom. However, most men, in the view of radical feminists, strive to maintain their dominance. Other feminists draw upon Marxist theory to explain the perpetuation of gender inequalities. In this view, women are subordinated within the family and left to undertake the tasks of bearing and rearing children in order to spare the ruling class the costs of "reproducing" the labor force. Thus, women's subordination is ensured. As a result, Engels and later Marxists believe that women's liberation will come about when capitalism and other forms of class society are replaced with socialism. The dismal situation of women in existing socialist societies has led many to reject this view. Another problem with Marxist forms of feminism is an inability of these theorists to establish causal links between historical and contemporary shifts in class relations to gender relations.

In the United States and in many other countries, feminism has had some real successes. Most women now consider a career their right if they should choose one; they demand and get equal pay for equal work; they are acquiring positions of power in government and business; they see themselves as equals with men both inside and outside the home. The basic concept in feminist ideology is one of equality, and women have made great strides towards that end.

Ferri, Enrico (1856-1928). Ferri, a student of Cesare Lombroso, expanded on the ideas of his teacher by claiming that social, economic, and political, as well as biological factors are involved in the causes of crime. In his book, *The Criminal Sociology,* he advocated restitution and other concepts of sociology as methods for dealing with crime and criminals.

Fielding, Henry (1707-1754). Although probably best known as the 18th century novelist who wrote *Tom Jones*, Henry Fielding might also be credited with laying the foundation for the first modern police force. The lawyer-novelist was appointed principal magistrate of Westminster, a city adjacent to central London, in 1748. He published the first crime survey in his 1750 article, "An Inquiry into the Causes of the Late Increase of Robberies." As principal magistrate, Fielding took over the police station located on Bow Street, London, and, with the help of his brother John, established what became the first known detective unit, the Bow Street Runners.

Fielding, John. A blind brother of Henry Fielding, held to the belief that lack of proper parenting and poverty were causes of juvenile delinquency. While acting in the capacity of magistrate, he sentenced young male offenders to service in the British Navy.

focal concerns. Walter Miller's "focal concern theory" held that the lower class subculture possess values or focal concerns that stress excitement, trouble, smartness, fate, and personal autonomy. These focal concerns are frequently in conflict with middle-class values and result in law violations (*See*: subcultural theory).

folk crime. H. Lawrence Ross referred to folk crime as the nonviolent, noncriminal behaviors that are reclassified as crime as the result of new regulations deemed necessary as society becomes more complex. Traffic violations, for example, are "folk crimes," yet the traffic offender does not typically achieve a negative public social image. Ross authored a 1982 book, *Deterring the Drunk Driver: Legal Policy and Social Control.*

folkways. Time honored ways of doing things. While they carry the force of tradition, their violation is unlikely to threaten the survival of the group. (See: folk crime; mores).

formal versus subterranean values. This is a conceptual dichotomy developed by David Matza and Graham Sykes to highlight differences in the systems of the dominant American culture and "deviant" youth groups, particularly delinquents.

They argued not only that society is divided into horizontal strata, but also that there is a vertical distinction based on two competing value systems. The *formal* values stress security, predictability, stability, deferred gratification, hard productive work, conformity, and long-range planning. The *subterranean* values stress excitement, experience, short-term hedonism, spontaneity, autonomy over one's own life, and a disdain for work. In conventional society the formal values govern daily behavior and the subterranean values are indulged in only in institutionalized form, for example, at holidays or festivals. Some groups, however, make the pursuit of the subterranean values the distinctive feature of their life-style.

Franklin, Benjamin (1706-1790). Franklin founded the American Philosophical Society in Philadelphia in 1743. He served as Pennsylvania's appointed agent to England and as a member of the second Continental Congress (1777) to draft the Declaration of Independence, which he signed. He was plenipotentiary to France and negotiated to obtain that country's help in the Revolution. He was also a noted statesman, scientist, and philosopher.

frankpledge. An ancient English system whereby members of a tithing, an association of 10 families, were bound together by a mutual pledge to keep the peace. Every male over the age of 12 was part of the system.

fraud. An act of trickery or deceit, especially involving misrepresentation.

free will. Associated with rational choice theory (classical theory). Holds that people are rational and weigh the benefits against the costs before choosing to act. Because criminals choose to violate the law, punishment is the appropriate crime control strategy.

Freud, Sigmund (1856-1939). One of the founders of modern psychology, noted as the originator of psychoanalysis.

Freud's published output was prodigious, and he continually modified and elaborated his theories throughout his career, making major alterations when he was 70 years of age. Basic to Freud's theories are the beliefs that much, if not most, of human behavior is unconsciously motivated and that neuroses often have their origins in early childhood memories or wishes that have subsequently been repressed. He developed an account of psychosexual development in which he stipulated that sexuality was present even in small infants, although the nature of this sexuality varied as the individual progressed through a sequence of stages to mature adult sexuality.

Freud also proposed a tripartite conceptual division of the self into the *id* (the reservoir of instinctual desires), and *ego* (the conscious self), and the *superego* (a form of conscience arising from socialization). The ego mediates between the pressures of the id and the superego in an effort to adapt the individual to the demands of the social world, and personality formation is largely the result of this process. Freud further believed that the workings of the unconscious mind could be made manifest by examining the content of dreams and slips of the tongue, by free-association techniques, and by prolonged personal interviews with patients conducted by trained analysts. Also central to Freud's theories is the concept of guilt.

Many of Freud's theories have been criticized on the grounds that they are culture-bound to nineteenth-century Vienna, are based on poor methodology, or are simply fanciful. His work remains a rich repository of fruitful insights, however, and continues to exert great influence, particularly in the United States.

frustration. The emotional state that occurs when a behavior is blocked.

frustration-aggression theory. Holds that frustration, which is a natural consequence of living, is a root cause of crime. Criminal behavior can be a form of adaptation when it results in stress reduction.

Fry, Elizabeth Gurney (1780-1845). She was born in Norwich, England and along with John Howard advocated reform in European prisons during the 19th century. She was an English Quaker women's prison reformer, who toured the United States and other countries in the early 1800s attempting to implement prison reforms. She encouraged separate facilities for female inmates, religious and secular education, improved classification systems for women, reintegrative and rehabilitative programs. A great deal of her work was also devoted to caring for the poor and neglected. In 1827, she published *Observations in Visiting, Superintendence and Government of Female Prisons*, which had a significant impact in reforming American prisons for women.

f-scale. This was designed to be an objective measure of fascist or authoritarian tendencies, developed in the 1930s by Ross Stagner. The measure is based on seven characteristic content areas that Stagner found in German and Italian fascist writings: nationalism, imperialism, militarism, racism, antiradicalism, middle-class consciousness, and a "strongman" philosophy of government and social control forces.

fuge. A rare dissociative state in which an individual, apparently forgetting who he or she is, goes to a new location either temporarily or permanently. Fuges have been associated with the mental illness of borderline personality disorder, or may be caused by extreme stress, leading to a conviction that escape is necessary. The term is derived from the Latin work for flight.

functional school, theory of crime. Emile Durkheim postulated that crime is normal, because research shows that crime exists in all societies and increases as society prospers, expands and progresses. The presence of crime, in fact, appears to have a correlate of a healthy society. Durkheim held that deviance may well be the way to social change. Contemporary American sociologist Kai T. Erikson reformulated Durkheim, clarifying the concept of deviance as "necessary" to social solidarity. Erikson argued, "It is deviant behavior that establishes and maintains the boundaries of acceptable behavior in society." (*See:* Durkheim).

futures research. A group of criminologists that study the likely futures as they impinge on crime and its control. It is a multidisciplinary branch of operations research whose principle aim is to facilitate long-range planning based on (1) forecasting from the past (demographics and crime statistics) supported by mathematical models; (2)

cross-disciplinary treatment of its subject matter; (3) systematic use of expert judgment, and; (4) a systems-analytical approach to its problems.

G

Gall, Franz Joseph (1758-1828). A German anatomist and physiologist who correctly identified the function of several areas of the brain and suggested these areas controlled or were related to certain parts of the body. Based on this assertion, he established the science of phrenology, the study of the external structure of the skull to determine the character of the individual (*See*: phrenology).

Galton, Francis (1812-1911). An English scientist and criminologist, Galton was a pioneer in the field of fingerprint science. Although he didn't develop a workable classification system, his work greatly aided Sir Edward Henry in his developments in this area of criminology.

gang. A group of individuals associated for some criminal, delinquent or other antisocial purpose.

Cloward and Ohlin's theory (*See*: differential opportunity theory)
Cohen's theory (*See*: subcultural theory)
Miller's theory (*See*: cultural deviance theory)

Garofalo, Raffaelo (1852-1934). The third major Italian positivist who developed the concept of "natural" crime. "Natural" crime consists of conduct that offends the basic moral sentiments of probity (respect for the property of others) and pity (revulsion against the voluntary infliction of suffering on others). In his major work, *Criminol-*

ogy, Garofalo outlined a theory of punishment which calls for elimination of those individuals unable to adapt to civilized life. (*See:* Beccaria; Lombroso).

Garrand, Rene (1849-1930). An advocate of the theory of rational social contracts, Garraud felt that individuals survey the pros and cons of their actions and then make their own rational choices. He argued that the principal instrument of social control should be the fear of pain and that punishment should be the principal method of creating fear to influence the will of the individual.

geographies. A demographical process that maps locations of groups relative to one another.

gender and crime. (*See:* hormones)

genetics. In criminology, the belief that criminality is inherited and runs in families. Early studies on the Jukes and Kallikak families were examples of early genetic theories that attempted to demonstrate how genetics operate to perpetuate deviancy. Another example of this type of biological theory is the XYY theory (*See:* XXY; Jukes; Kallikak).

gentrification. This is a process of reclaiming and refurbishing deteriorated houses and depressed neighborhoods for resale.

ghetto. A neighborhood or portion of a city where the predominant population is made up by one ethnic group who are restricted by economic pressure or social discrimination.

Giambattista della Porta (1536-1615). May have been the world's first criminologist. Giambattista made anthropometric measurements in order to establish a typology and was a practitioner of physiogonomics (interpreting the significance of relationships between the body and mind.)

glandular theory. This theory links abnormal, antisocial, deviant, or criminal behavior with thyroidal, adrenal, or other glandular dysfunctions.

Glueck, Sheldon (1898-1972) and Eleanor. American criminologists. This husband and wife team wrote many articles on criminal character and behavior. Their most famous study was *Five Hundred Criminal Careers*, first published in 1930.

Goodard, Henry H. He studied institutionalized "feeble-minded" individuals in the 1920s. He concluded that a majority of juvenile delinquents were feebleminded. These studies were latter discounted for their lack of scientific rigor. He authored, *The Kallikak Family: A Study in the Heredity of Feeblemindedness* (1912).

Goring, Charles Buckman (1870-1919). A British research scientist and prison physician. Goring published a statistical study of 3,000 male convicts entitled *The English Convict*, in which he claimed criminal tendencies are related to mental deficiencies and psychological factors rather than to physical characteristics as theorized by Cesare Lombroso.

gossip. The means of social control generated by verbal assault or comment, usually expressed to a person not the object of the conversation or assault.

grand jury. Panels of private citizens that decide whether indictments for alleged crimes are warranted. As an oversight group some grand juries also launch investigations into affairs in a community, such as public corruption, gambling, and prostitution.

Guerry, Andre-Michel (1802-1866). He assisted in the establishment of the cartographic school of criminology, which posited that social factors, including gender and age, significantly influenced crime rates. Other factors such as season, climate, population composition and density along with poverty were directly correlated with social deviance and criminality.

H

habeas corpus. A written court order to bring the accused before the court.

habitual criminal statutes. Laws that require long prison sentences for offenders found to be career criminals. An example are the "Three Strikes" laws that have been passed in many states and the federal system. In California, an offender convicted of a third serious felony and prosecuted under this statute must receive a sentence of 25 years to life. Habitual offender statutes are generally a form of mandatory minimums that do not allow the judge discretion.

halo effect. A tendency on the part of a person to be unduly influenced by positive traits or characteristics of another person. Thus, in evaluating or judging another, the perceiver's estimates of other aspects of the person's functioning and personality are (often without awareness) made to coincide with the most prominent impression.

Hammurabic Code. Referred to as the first written laws. It dealt with criminal acts and penalties while attempting to control certain daily aspects of life. The punishment was harsh and was based on the concept of *lex talionis* which equates to the biblical "eye for an eye."

hands off doctrine. A judicial policy that believes that the courts should not interfere with the operation of prisons. A shift to judicial activism occurred during the liberal era of the Warren Supreme Court, however then shifted back to a hands-off approach under the Burger and Rehnquist courts.

hate crime. Criminal acts in which individuals are victimized because of race, religion, sexual orientation, ethnicity or national origin. The Hate Crime Statistics Act (Public Law 101-275) was enacted in 1990. The act requires the Justice Department to acquire data on hate crimes and to publish an annual summary of findings. The FBI has incorporated the hate-crime data into its current Uniform Crime Report. On June 11, 1993, the U.S. Supreme Court unanimously upheld the constitutionality of a Wisconsin hate crime penalty-enhancement law in *Wisconsin v. Mitchell.*

Haviland, John (1792-1852). A famous penal-architecture reformer, Haviland built the state prisons in New Jersey and Pennsylvania. He designed such innovations as detached exercise yards, cell doors opening into corridors, and two-story wings.

hedonistic calculus (also utilitarianism). English reformer Jeremy Bentham developed the theory of utilitarianism or "hedonistic calculus," which attempted to explain all human behavior through the process of rewards and punishments. A major proponent of the Classical School of Criminology, Bentham saw criminality as a result of a person's attempt to achieve the greatest pleasure or happiness while minimizing pain or discomfort. According to Bentham, people are constantly calculating the potential pleasure and punishments of their actions. People are thought to possess free will and therefore the criminal law ought to be organized in such a way that the offender will experience more pain than the pleasure derived from his or her criminal behavior.

heredity. Biological traits passed from parent to child or generation to generation.

histrionic personality disorder. Traits include excessive emotionality and attention seeking, inappropriately sexually provocative or seductive behavior.

Hobbes, Thomas (1588-1679). One of the world's greatest philosophers, Hobbes believed in utilitarian punishment for a violation of the law. Punishment was not to be vengeful and must be in proportion to the crime committed. Hobbes also stated that punishment must be preceded by public condemnation and inflicted by the proper authority and, as its end, must dispose individuals to obey the law.

Holmes-Rahe Social Readjustment Scale. A scale used to rate the probability of suicide. The scale rank orders a series of 43 stressful life events and applies to each event a value. A total of 200 or more points is indicative of a suicide candidate or of suicide in a questionable death case.

homicide. The unlawful killing of a human being. Usually called willful homicide, which refers to intentionally causing the death of another, without legal justification. Justifiable homicide, in contrast, is a legal defense permitted by law.

Hooton, Earnest Albert (1887-1954). An American physical anthropologist, Hooton conducted studies to ascertain whether criminals differ physically from law-abiding citizens of the same race, nationality, and economic status. He believed that biological determinism influenced an individual's criminal tendencies.

hospice. Generally, a final resting place for the terminally ill.

Hospice of San Michele. This was a multipurpose facility created in the early 18th century in Rome, Italy. The unit housing juveniles was a prototype of early adult and juvenile systems in the United States. The cellular design is considered to be its significant contribution.

house arrest. A sentence, usually a condition of probation, whereby the judge orders the defendant restricted to home. The offender is usually allowed to leave during certain hours for employment, medical, and church attendance. House arrest can be monitored by electronic monitoring technology.

Howard, John (1726-1790). He is considered the "father of the penitentiary." The name of John Howard, High Sheriff of Bedfordshire for almost two decades, became synonymous with English prison reform. His work, *State of Prisons*, was based on observations of prison conditions throughout England and continental Europe and influenced the passage of the Penitentiary Act of 1779. This legislation resulted in England's first penitentiary, one that incorporated many principles of basic prison reform.

hypoglycemia. A condition that may occur in susceptible individuals when the level of blood sugar falls below an acceptable range, causing anxiety, headaches, confusion, fatigue, and aggressive behavior.

hypothesis. A proposition set forth as an explanation for some specified phenomenon.

I

Id. That aspect of the personality from which drives, wishes, urges, and desires emanate. More formally, the division of the psyche associated with instinctual impulses and demands for immediate satisfaction of primitive needs.

illegitimate opportunities structures. Subcultural pathways (ways and means) to success that are disapproved of by the wider society. These opportunity structures, according to some scholars, are not always available when legitimate opportunities are closed.

imitation. Learning through copying the behavior of another person. Garbriel Tarde pointed out at the beginning of the 19th century that the structure and norms of society can be traced, in large part, to our tendency to follow the behavior prescribed by others.

importation model. The belief that inmates bring their values, attitudes, and behaviors from the outside community. In this model, prisons are violent places because most inmates are poor, minority, and come from the lower classes where violence is a way of life. Those values of violence are simply brought into the prison (*See*: deprivation model).

impression management. The intentional enactment of practiced behavior that is intended to convey to others one's desirable personal traits and social qualities.

impulsivity. A trait characterized by acting without regard to consequences. Persons who are impulsive tend to be at high risk for school problems, delinquency, promiscuity, and drug use.

incarceration. The imprisonment of an adjudicated offender in a correctional institution.

incapacitation. A major purpose of criminal sanctions: to protect society by incarcerating the offender (*See*: incarceration).

index offenses. These comprise the eight Part 1 offenses reported by the FBI in the annual *Uniform Crime Reports*: willful homicide, arson, forcible rape, robbery, burglary, aggravated assault, larceny, and motor vehicle theft.

indeterminate sentence. Refers to sentence lengths determined by correctional policy rather than by the courts or legislature. An offender receives an open-ended sentence (e.g., one to ten years); the actual time served depends on the inmate's behavior and other conditions established by correctional policy. A parole board or authority determines when to release the offender on supervision associated with the rehabilitation model.

indictment. A formal charge by a grand jury.

indirect control. A behavioral influence that arises from an individual's identification with noncriminals and his or her desire to conform to societal norms.

inequality. (*See*: social inequality; unjust law)

inferiority complex. A term first used by Alfred Adler to describe an individual's sense that he or she is not equal in competence to other people and is inadequate to meet the demands of the environment. An individual might attempt to compensate for feelings of inferiority by concealing them through feats of courage and achievement. Thus, a person who feels socially inadequate might strive to become successful in a highly profiled endeavor. In extreme forms, efforts at compensation may result in aggressive or antisocial behavior.

inmate subculture. The values, attitudes, and behaviors that are contained within the prison setting.

insanity. A defense against criminal charges, which, if proven, can result in a finding of innocence because of the inability of the accused to form criminal intent as a result of mental illness (*See*: Durham rule; M'Naghten rule).

instrumental Marxism. Part of the Marxist School of thought, which postulates that the state is used by the wealthy and powerful to control the underclass. The elite or ruling classes influence the creation of laws that serve their interests (*See*: class conflict).

integrated theory. This theoretical model seeks to expand and synthesize earlier positions into a modern analytical device with explanatory and predictive abilities. This is an attempt to blend seemingly independent variables and concepts into a coherent explanation of crime.

intelligence. The capacity for learning, reasoning and understanding. The term includes aptitude (mental alertness) in grasping truths, relationships, facts, and meanings. An intelligence quotient is an intelligence test score that is obtained by dividing mental age, which reflects the age-graded level or performance as derived from population norms, by chronological age and multiplying by 100: a score of 100 thus indicates a performance at exactly the normal level for that age group.

interactionist theory. A key sociological perspective in criminology that focuses on the way in which crime is generated by social control agencies (i.e. the criminal justice system) as they attach stigmatizing labels to individual offenders, who often "live up" to the criminal identify that flows from labels, and who devote themselves to criminal careers.

intensive-supervision probation. An intermediate sanction or alternative to prison for convicted nonviolent offenders who ordinarily would not be candidates for regular probation or who require closer monitoring. The offenders are generally assigned to specific probation officers having smaller case loads which allows for increased supervision.

institutionalization. The acquisition or internalization of prison values, attitudes, and behaviors as a result of long-term incarceration. Institutionalization is the socialization process whereby inmates adapt to the regimentation, degradation, and loss of autonomy which often occur with imprisonment. Institutionalization is frequently a major obstacle in community adjustment and reintegration. It frequently contributes to further criminal behavior and a return to prison.

internalized control. Self-regulation of behavior and conformity to societal norms as a result of guilt feelings arising in the conscience.

involuntary manslaughter. A homicide in which the perpetrator unintentionally but recklessly causes the death of another person by consciously taking a grave risk that endangers the person's life.

Irish system. A system of punishment, developed by Sir William Crofton, that provided for progressive stages in a prison term and for release under supervision before final termination of sentence. Represents an early form of parole.

J

jail. A facility, usually operated by the county sheriff, empowered to detain pretrial defendants, sentenced offenders committed for periods of less than one year, and sentenced inmates awaiting transfer to state prison.

Johari window. A theoretical model for explaining the concept of an individual's interpersonal disclosure and feedback. The model consists of four quadrants: (1) public self (known by individual and others); (2) blind self (known by others but unknown by the individual); private self (known only by the individual); and (4) unknown area (information of which neither the individual nor others are aware).

Jukes family. The case name given to a New York State family with a notable record for retardation, delinquency, and crime. A study published in 1875 (Richard L. Dugdale) reported that more than 2,000 men and women "of Jukes book" had been traced. Of these, 171 were classified as criminals, 458 were behind their age groups in school, and hundreds of others were labeled paupers, intemperates, and harlots. Like the record of the Kallikak family, the story of the Jukes was taken as proof (since challenged) that heredity is a dominant factor in development.

Jung, Carl Gustav (1875-1961). A Swiss psychotherapist who held that, in addition to the individual unconscious, there is a basic *collective unconscious*, consisting of the living symbols and images shared by all mankind that emerge in dreams, fantasies, delusions, and myths. These emotionally charged archetypes, or collectives images, express fundamental aspects of human experience. Jung saw man as striving for individualization or self-realization, a psychic wholeness reconciling the tension of complementary opposites in personality. Among the opposed tendencies are the two attitudes of *introversion* versus *extroversion*, which respectively direct attention to inner and outer worlds, and the four functions of *sensing* versus *intuiting* as ways of knowing, and *feeling* versus *thinking* as ways of evaluation. Exaggeration of any of these *psychological types* or orientations in ego consciousness causes its opposite to become more powerful in the unconscious.

Psychic wholeness requires their creative synthesis through personal transformation and self-discovery.

just deserts. A philosophy of justice which asserts that the punishment should fit the crime and the culpability of the offender. This model is associated with classical and rational choice theory (*See*: retribution).

justice model. A conservative approach to the purposes of incarceration. The model's goals are to legally and humanely control the offender, to provide adequate care and custody, to offer voluntary treatment, and to protect society. This approach views confinement as punishment and does not place great emphasis on rehabilitation. A school of thought that feels justice is served when criminals are administered punishment proportional to the severity of the offense (*See*: just deserts; retribution).

justice of the peace. Originally (established in 1326) a man, usually of the lower nobility, who was assigned to investigate and try minor cases. Presently a judge of a lower local or municipal court with limited jurisdiction.

justice, sporting theory of. A term applied to the contentious method of judicial procedure in criminal trials. In this method, characteristic of criminal procedure derived from Anglo-Saxon precedents, the prosecution presents all the damaging evidence and the defense all the favorable, while the function of the judge is to act as umpire to see that the game is played fairly, according to the rules of procedure laid down in the law and in court decisions (*See*: adversary system).

justifiable homicide. A homicide, permitted by law, in defense of a legal right or mandate.

Justinian Code. Authored in A.D. 529 by Emperor Justinian of the Byzantine Empire, this code became the standard of law in Europe during the Middle Ages. The code was compiled by selecting all useful sections of all the existing or known codes and constitutions of the time.

juvenile delinquent. A youth, usually under 18 years of age, who has been adjudicated in a juvenile court of committing an offense in violation of the criminal or penal code or who has been found in juvenile court to have committed an act in violation of criminal statutes.

juvenile justice system. A distinct court system separate from the adult system. Based on the concept of *parens patriae*, or the state as parent, which holds to the principle that the government has an obligation to assure that children are properly cared for. Juvenile proceedings are informal and generally nonadversarial. Juveniles are entitled to most due process rights afforded adults. However, they do not have a right to bail or to a jury trial.

K

Kallikak family. The case name of a family study by the American psychologist Henry H. Goddard in his search for the causes of mental retardation. Impressed by Sir Francis Galton's theory that genius is hereditary, Goddard reasoned that he same might be true of deficiency. While director of the Vineland Training School for Feebleminded Children, he noticed that one of the inmates and various abnormal individuals in that part of New Jersey had the same name as a prominent and respected family. Goddard was able to trace the ancestry of both groups to a soldier in the Revolutionary War, whom he called Martin Kallikak

(Kallikak is from Greek, meaning good-bad). Martin had an illegitimate son by a girl described as retarded. Of 480 descendants who could be traced, 143 were classed as defective and 46 as normal. The rest were not labeled, but illegitimacy, crime, alcoholism, and mental disorders were reported to be common throughout the group. Martin later married and started a family tree in which only three of 496 traced descendants were classed as defective, while many were eminent.

In *The Kallikak Family* (1912) Goddard maintained that his study proved the primary role of heredity as a cause of mental deficiency. His findings, however have been questioned on several grounds, such as definition of terms, objectivity and the role of environment.

Khadi justice. An arbitrary type of law, described by German philosopher Max Weber (1864-1920), that is based on religious precepts rather than procedural rules, as in the Islamic Sharia courts. Under the Islamic system, criminal law consisted of the personal decisions of the sultan, based on local variations of custom and belief. Weber described Khadi justice as one of the three types of administration of justice, the other two being empirical and rational. He describes the Anglo-American system as mainly empirical (relying on analogies and precedents) with some elements of Khadi justice (tradition and individual justice).

kidnapping. The transportation or confinement of a person without authority of law and without his or her consent, or without the consent of his or her guardian, if a minor.

kinship. A relationship through adoption, blood, or marriage.

Kretschmer, Ernst (1888-1964). A German psychiatrist who thought mental disorders and crime were related. He felt that a psychotic individual should be given medical treatment, not confinement in jails. He is considered the father of psychopharmacology, the science concerned with the relationship of drugs to human behavior.

Kriminalpolitik. The political handling of crime, or a criminology-based social policy.

L

labeling theory. Frank Tannenbaum in 1938 defined the beginning of a criminal career as the result of a "dramatization of evil"—the point at which a child is singled out from the group and treated as a delinquent. By 1963 Howard Becker had further developed and renamed Tannenbaums's theory. Now called labeling, Becker's theory held that this interactionist concept could explain deviance in terms of societal reaction to acts of the individual. Labeling theory has come into prominence over the past two decades as a major approach to explaining the nature of deviance. The labeling theory stresses that social rules are not clear-cut and that they result in ambiguous evaluations of behavior. Deviance is also emphasized as a process in which deviant rules and self-conceptions are shaped. Becker held that the stigma attached to the label (delinquent, ex-convict, thief) would contribute to a self-fulfilling prophecy or further crime (*See:* Self-fulfilling prophecy).

larceny-theft. The unlawful taking or attempted taking of property other than a motor vehicle from the possession of another, by stealth, without force and without deceit, with intent to permanently deprive the owner of the property.

latency theory. A psychological concept, developed in particular by Sigmund Freud and his followers, that postulates the existence of urges, needs, and potential behavior that are not manifested in overt conduct, but exist on an unconscious level and are likely to emerge unless redirected by outside (therapeutic) intervention.

Lavater, Johan Casper (1741-1801). A Swiss scholar and theologian, Lavater published a four-volume work on physiognomy called *Physiognomical Fragments*, which made extravagant claims about the alleged relation between facial features and human conduct. His writings were the forerunners of the physiognomy theories of Cesare Lombroso and others (*See:* physiognomy).

law, customary. Social practices or norms that have been codified into the penal code. Law in this sense is the result of common usage, not of legislation, and is generally considered to be the laymen's rules concerning matters of everyday life. Customary law developed with certain class changes in feudal society. Whereas feudal law covered the nobles and peasants, customary law arose to cover merchants and tradesmen. Trade customs formed its basis, and it was further developed by judicial decision. To be valid, a custom had to be public, of long use, and for the public good. When no valid custom existed, the judge made a ruling, and it eventually became custom.

Law, Elizabethan Poor. A law enacted by the English Parliament in 1603, summarizing and consolidating a variety of laws concerning poor relief passed during the preceding century. The law required the local community to assume responsibility for the care of its own poor, established the principle of destitution as a test of eligibility for assistance, and decreed that relief could be granted only in return for work in places provided for housing the poor. The principles of public assistance established by the Elizabethan Poor Law governed the administration of relief in England and the United States for over 300 years.

law, natural. An abstract concept of law based on the relation among God, man, and nature. An ideal higher than positive or man-made law, it forms the basis of justice in the ethical sense. It embodies such ideas as the existence of a universal order governing all people and the inalienable rights of the individual. John Locke used natural law principles in setting forth the basic rights of the individual in his social contract theories, and natural law ideas were influential in the framing of the Constitution of the United States.

law of effect. A fundamental concept in learning theory holding that, all others things being equal, a person will more readily learn those habits leading to satisfaction and will not learn (or will learn with greater difficulty) those habits leading to dissatisfaction.

laws of imitation. An explanation of crime as learned behavior. Individuals are thought to emulate behavior patterns of others with whom they have contact. People are more likely to imitate those whom they admire. Reverse imitation may occur if the model is not respected (*See*: Tarde).

learning theory. An explanation of crime and delinquency postulating that criminal behavior, like legal and normative behavior, is learned. Such learning may be acquired from those already engaged in illegal activity, as in differential association theory; learning may be reinforced through rewards and punishments. The three schools of learning theory are: (1) classical conditioning; (2) operant conditioning; and (3) cognitive learning theory. (1) and (2) focus on the stimulus-response connection as the basic unit of analysis in the learning process; (3) suggests that conditioning and learning are one and the same.

legalization. The removal of all criminal penalties for an act that was previously against the law (*See*: decriminalization).

legitimate opportunity. (*See*: operant conditioning; classical learning).

lex talionis. Law of the claw. (1) Law of retaliation, such as "an eye for an eye and a tooth for a tooth." (2) In modern times, also the acts of one nation in retaliation for the acts of another, which may include peaceful but still retaliatory acts.

liberal criminology. The cornerstone of liberal or positivistic philosophy has been the concept of rehabilitation, and the reintegration of offenders into mainstream society. Liberal criminology supports the due process model and community-shared responsibilities towards crime control. In the area of punishment there is a trend towards community-oriented corrections, education, occupational training and outreach programs. (*See*: conservative criminology and radical criminology)

liberal feminist theory. Freda Adler in *Sisters in Crime* and Rita Simon in *The Contemporary Woman and Crime* have asserted that low crime rates among females are due to their lower economic and social position. They further state that over time and with increased rights and opportunity crime rates for both men and women will converge. (*See:* Marxist feminists)

liquor law violations. In offense reporting, the term includes all state or local liquor law violations, except drunken-

ness and driving under the influence. Federal violations
are also excluded.

Liszt, Franz von (1851-1919). Cousin of the composer of the
same name; best remembered for theories that he termed
the global science of criminal law (Gesamte
Strafrechtswissenschaft), and the twofold division of
criminals into criminals of the moment
(Augenblicksverbrecher) and chronicle criminals
(Zussandverbrecher).

Locke, John (1632-1704). An English philosopher, Locke supposed that people came to an agreement, or a social contract, with one another to surrender their individual rights
of judging and punishment, not to a king, but to the community as a whole. He also advocated that, should the
sovereign government violate any of the laws, the community has the right to withdraw from that authority. His
major works include *Two Treatises of Government* (1690)
and *An Essay Concerning Human Understanding* (1690).

Lombroso, Cesare (1835-1909). Italian criminologist and professor of psychiatry, and later of criminal anthropology,
at the University of Turin. Lombroso is considered the
father of modern criminology and the original spokesman
for the positivist viewpoint. In his book *The Criminal Man*,
he maintained that the criminal type can be identified by
a number of different physical characteristics. He believed
that the victim should be compensated by the criminal
and that society should be protected from degenerate and
atavistic criminal types. He also advocated the use of indeterminate sentences, but favored the death penalty as a
last resort. Contemporary criminologists have criticized
his restricted notion of crime and criminal behavior, claiming that, because he focused primarily on the perpetrators
of violent crimes against the person, he failed to develop

a meaningful theory that would also explain why intelligent people of "normal" appearance and affluent status happen to engage—sometimes routinely—in property crimes, which often require complex legal, business, or organizational skills. (*See:* Goring, Charles; Lavater, Johan; Tarde, Gabriel)

longitudinal study. An analysis, conducted repeatedly over a period of time, that focuses on studies of a particular group.

looking-glass self. This concept was suggested by Charles Horton Cooley as the process whereby an individual develops identify or self-concept. According to Cooley, individuals come to know or define themselves through the process of internalizing their perceptions of how they think others, especially significant others, around them perceive them. They come to adopt or accept as their own those valuations, definitions, and judgments of themselves and what they believe is seen "reflected" in the faces of others in their social environment. It is, the individual's conception of the perceived responses toward that individual, rather than the actual responses of others, that is the essential element in the process of self-development.

The process is especially important in the early years of a child. The resultant self, then, is a social product involving three components: the *actual* response of others toward the individual; the related *perceived* responses of others toward the individual; and the individual's *internalization* of these perceived responses. In this final step, individuals come to define and distinguish themselves, or to create a self congruent with those social definitions and judgments of them made by significant others in their social environment.

lust murder. A form of homicide that is primarily motivated by aberrant sexual fantasies.

M

Machiavelli, Niccolo (1469-1527). An Italian statesman, who advocated in his book *The Prince* that it was the duty of a ruler to furnish his subjects an example of moral goodness and patriotism. He felt that in the pursuit of political good, the ends justified the means, and his diplomacy took no account of honesty or morals in arrangements with other people as long as they were for the common good of the community.

Mack, Julian W. (1866-1943). A federal judge for 30 years, Mack ranks as one of the foremost innovators of juvenile justice. Born in San Francisco, he received his law degree at Harvard and went into practice in Chicago in 1890. He was elected to a judgeship for the Circuit Court of Cook County, Illinois, in 1903; between 1904 and 1907, he presided over Chicago's Juvenile Court, the first in the world (established by the Illinois legislature in 1899). Under Mack, the court dealt with neglected and abused children, runaways, school dropouts, and juveniles who had committed crimes. Mack supported the founding of the National Probation Officers Association. In 1907, he was promoted to the Illinois Appeals Court, and in 1911 he was appointed by President Taft to a seat on the U.S. Court of Appeals for the Seventh Circuit, from which he retired in 1941.

Maconochie, Alexander (1787-1860). He is considered "the father of parole." Maconochie was born in Edinburgh, Scotland. As head of the British penal colony at Norfolk Island, he established an early form of parole in 1840. The system rewarded positive behavior and allowed inmates to earn marks and thereby to progress through a series of confinement stages resulting in conditional freedom with a ticket-of-leave and, finally, absolute freedom. He held two views regarding penological theory: (1) punishment should not be vindictive but aimed at reform; and (2) a sentence should be indeterminate, with release depending on prisoner's industriousness and effort rather than on time served. Returning to England in 1844 to campaign for penal reform, he was appointed governor of the new Birmingham Borough Prison in 1849. He was unable to institute his reforms because he was dismissed from his position in 1851 by visiting justices who had power over the prison, on grounds that his methods were too lenient.

macrosociological study. The study of overall social arrangements, their structures, and their long-term effects.

male in se. (Latin., lit. bad in itself) Crimes have been divided, according to their nature into crimes *mala in se* and crimes *mala prohibita*. The former comprise those acts that are immoral or wrong in themselves, such a murder, rape, arson, burglary, larceny, breach of the peace, forgery, and the like. (*See: mala prohibita*)

mala prohibita. Those crimes that are made illegal by legislation (gambling, prostitution, drug use) as opposed to acts that are crimes because they are considered evil in and of themselves, or *mala in se*.

malice aforethought. The *mens rea* requirement for murder, consisting of the intention to kill with the awareness that there is no right to kill.

mandatory minimum sentences. A sentencing structure that allows no discretion for certain crimes. For example, in the federal system, possession of more than five grams of crack cocaine requires the court to impose a minimum sentence of at least 10 years.

manslaughter. Criminal homicide without malice, committed intentionally after provocation (voluntary manslaughter) or recklessly (involuntary manslaughter).

Martinson, Robert. Along with Douglas Lipton and Judith Wilks, Martinson reviewed 231 studies on treatment and concluded that by and large rehabilitation was ineffective. They developed the premise that rehabilitative efforts of correctional programs has not worked.

Marxist theory. Marxist conflict theory originated about 1848 with the publication of *The Communist Manifesto*. The main element of this theory is that crime develops as a result of the economic factors and a struggle between the classes. A capitalist system, according to Marx, emphasizes profit driven by competition. This school views society being made up of diverse groups who have competing interests and therefore are in perpetual competition or conflict with each other; that group(s) possessing the most power are able to use the law and the criminal justice system to protect their interests. Criminal laws, created by the affluent and powerful, are designed to protect the "haves" from the "have-nots." Marxist criminologists will often emphasize the disparity in punishment received by lower classes, usually minorities, with those received by the powerful upper classes. They point to the overwhelming lower-class prison population to reinforce their position. Revolution to eliminate capitalism and replace it with a socialistic system is the only way, according to this theory, to control crime.

Marxist feminists theory. A view that gender inequality stems from the unequal power of men in a capitalist society. Women are exploited by husbands and fathers. Female criminality is in response to the subordination of women and male aggression and exploitation.

Maslow, Abraham H. (1908-1970). American personality theorist. In 1951, he became increasingly involved in the emerging field of humanistic psychology theory. His theories concerning human development and motivation and his writings about self-actualization made him one of the leading figures in modern psychology. Maslow's work is a cornerstone of much of industrial psychology. Although he aimed "to show that human beings are capable of something grander than war and prejudice and hatred," it has been argued that Maslow's theories are more applicable to humanity's affairs and achievements than as general descriptions of human motivation.

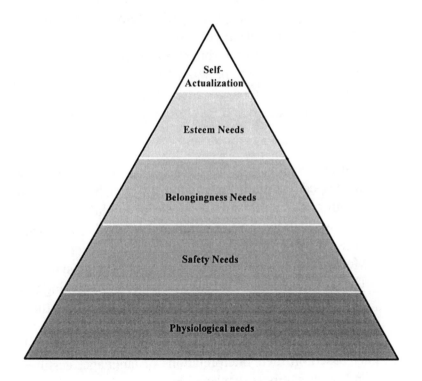

Chart showing Maslow's hierarchy of needs.

mass murder. The killing of three or more persons in one time and in one place.

Maudsley, Henry (1835-1918). A renowned English physician at the age of 21 who was appointed medical superintendent of the Manchester Royal Lunatic Asylum at age 23. At 27, he was editing the *Journal of Mental Science* and, at 34, was appointed professor of Medical Jurisprudence at University College in London. He paid particular attention to the borderline area between insanity and crime. He applied knowledge from other fields to the problem of criminal behavior, with awareness of the effect environmental factors had in the causes of crime. He opposed the harsh punishment of criminals, although his argument against unjust punishment was weakened by his inability to differentiate control from punishment. In 1847 he published *Responsibility in Mental Diseases*. This work remains much debated, because Maudsley argues against the popular idea that a truly insane person acts without motive.

Mead, George Herbert (1863-1931). This noted sociologist developed Symbolic Interactionism, which stresses behavior as a function not only of social conditions but also of how the individual interprets and responds to the reactions of others in his or her environment. According to Mead, people communicate or interact through symbols. These symbols can be language, gestures, or anything that represents something else. The person interprets these symbolic interactions and forms opinions about his or her own actions. Individuals judge themselves and their reality based on their interpretations of language, gestures, and other symbols displayed by others. In other words, people come to judge themselves and their behaviors based on how other people react and respond to them. Labeling theory derives its ideas from this school of thought (*See*: labeling theory).

medical model. A penalogical concept that suggests that prisoners are mentally or physically "sick" and that confinement is a "cure." Offenders are sentenced to prison to be treated and rehabilitation. The medical model in criminal justice need not include confinement. The major goal is whether in or out of custody is simply to implement a treatment plan after a diagnosis has been established.

medicalization of crime and deviance. Decriminalizing certain acts and attempting to control them and their perpetrators socially with medical institutions, rather than with the criminal justice system.

mens rea. (Latin) One of the two elements of every crime, which are the criminal act or omission and the mental element or criminal intent, the *mens rea*. The latter is the state of mind that accompanies the particular act defined as criminal. Hence, the *mens rea* of each crime will be different. For instance, in the crime of receiving stolen goods, it means acknowledging that the goods were stolen; in the case of murder, malice aforethought; in the case of theft, an intention to steal.

Merton, Robert King (1910 -). A U.S. Sociologist, Merton was a professor of Sociology at Columbia University since 1941, he has been an influential sociologist theorist in such areas as structural analysis and the sociology of science. Among his many books are *Social Theory and Social Structure* (1949), *On the Shoulders of Giants* (1965), *Sociological Ambivalence and Other Essays* (1976), *Toward a Metric of Science* (1977), and the *Sociology of Science in Europe* (1977).

mesomorph. One of three body-builds or somatotypes developed by William Sheldon. Sheldon believed that criminals display distinct body types that make them more prone towards criminality. The mesomorph was a type which is muscular, athletic, active, triangular-shaped and somewhat aggressive. The individual is also gregarious, assertive, and action-oriented and often involved in committing crime.

Mesopotamian laws and codes. The earliest signs of well-developed written law codes emerged from early cultures in Mesopotamia, the land bordered by the Tigris and Euphrates rivers. Although early Sumerian codes, no doubt, existed as far back as 3000 B.C., the Babylonian Code of Hammurabi is the most famous. (*See:* Hammurabic Code)

microsociological study. The study of everyday patterns of behavior and personal interactions.

middle-class measuring rod. Concept used by Albert Cohen in his "Theory of Delinquent Subcultures" to describe the dominant values, attitudes, and behaviors of middle-class society. According to Cohen, youth socialized in lower-class culture are unable to meet the standards of middle-class society and become frustrated. This frustration lead to a type of reaction formation wherein lower class youth turn middle-class values upside down and become involved in behavior considered malicious, negativistic, and non-utilitarian.

Minimal brain dysfunction (MBD). An attention-deficit disorder that may produce such asocial behavior as impulsivity, hyperactivity, and aggressiveness.

Minnesota Multiphasic Personality Inventory (MMPI). The most widely used personality inventory developed by R.

Starke Hathaway and J. Charnley McKinley. The test has a number of subscales that measure distinct personality traits including psychopathic deviation (Pd scale), schizophrenia (Sc scale), and hypomania (ma scale). The MMPI has been used to predict the propensity of criminal behavior and has been widely used as a screening instrument for potential criminal justice applicants.

Elio Monachesi and Hathaway indicated that scores on some of these scales, especially the psychopathic deviation scale have been found to predict criminality.

M'Naghten rule. A test of insanity used in the United States. To be used in court as a defense, it must be established that at the time of the crime the offender was suffering from such a mental disability that he or she did not have the capacity to know the difference between right and wrong (*See*: insanity; Durham rule).

misdemeanor. A minor criminal act or infraction typically punished by a small fine, probation or less than one year in the county jail.

modeling. A term to describe the process of imitation, also known as learning by observation. Modeling is considered a very important aspect of socialization. A child learns what types of behavior are positive, appropriate and approved by parents and society in general. Various characteristics of models increase the likelihood that children will imitate them. Three of the most important are a high degree of nurturance displayed by the model toward the child, power to reward others, including the child, and a high frequency of interaction between the child and the model. Conversely, children raised without positive role models can become maladjusted, and as a result, often at odds with mainstream society.

monopoly. When a corporation has no competition in a particular market (*See*: shared monopoly).

monopoly capitalism. The historical stage of capitalization predicted by Karl Marx in which fewer and fewer firms become larger and larger, dominating the economy and eliminating competition.

monotheism. Belief in one god.

monozyotic (MZ) twins. As opposed to dizygotic (or DZ) twins, MZ twins develop from the same egg and carry virtually the same genetic material.

Montero, Pedro Dorado (1861-1919). A professor who fought against traditional criminological ideas and systems of his time. Dorado is considered the pioneer of the penal sanction as a moral, spiritual function.

Montesquieu: Charles Louis de Seconat, Baron de la Brede et de Montesquieu (1689-1755). A French lawyer, philosopher, and man of letters, who epitomized the Enlightenment's concern for the rights of humanity. His book *The Spirit of the Laws,* and essay "Persian Letters," condemned the barbarous injustice of the French penal code and advocated reforms that would make punishments less severe and more adapted to the crimes for which they were imposed.

motion. An oral or written request to a judge that asks the court to make a specified ruling, finding, decision, or order. It may be presented at any appropriate moment from arrest until the end of the trial.

moral development theory. A view that criminality is caused by individuals who have underdeveloped morals and value judgments. This hinders them in making rationale choices between right and wrong.

moral enterprise. A term that encompasses all the efforts a particular interest group makes to have its sense of propriety enacted into law.

moral turpitude. Baseness or depravity of conduct; to be without moral value.

mores. Behavioral proscriptions covering potentially serious violations of a group's values, and would probably include strictures against *mala in se* crimes (murder, rape, and robbery).

More, Sir Thomas (1478-1535). English statesman and author who wrote in his book *Utopia* that criminality is a reflection of society. Utopia was a city where More saw all the policies and institutions governed completely by reason. He also fought for religious freedom, denying the head of state, Henry VIII, supreme power over religious matters, a fight that cost More his life.

motivation. The underlying goal or reason for the actions of an individual or group of individuals.

multiple personality disorder. This is the rarest dissociative disorder, in which the person shifts between two or more distinct patterns of behavior that are often oppositional to one another. It is a pathological condition resulting from the splitting off of an unacceptable segment of the personality by means of disassociation. Thus, certain aspects and functions of the personality are removed from the conscious control of the individual and tend to act as a separate or secondary personality. One personality dominates at a time, and the individual may not be aware of other personalities. Multiple personality disorder should not be confused with schizophrenia, which literally means "split mind" but does not refer to multiple patterns of behavior. One of the most recent example is William (Billy) Stanley Milligan, who, at the time of his 1977 arrest for raping three women in Columbus, Ohio, was discovered to have at least 10 distinct personalities. After he was found not guilty by reason of insanity—the first time that this ruling was made for a case of multiple personality—another 13 personalities were discovered.

motor vehicle theft. The unlawful taking or attempted taking of a vehicle owned by another, with the intent of depriving him or her of it, permanently or temporarily.

Murton, Thomas (1928-1990). Criminologist-penologist and professor who attempted to reform the corruption of the Arkansas penal system in the late 1960s. He was fired for his efforts and was ostracized from corrections. He became a professor at the University of Minnesota, Dept. of Criminal Justice Administration for several years. He authored two books and numerous articles on the Arkansas Prison Scandal. The movie "Brubaker," was based upon his book, *Accomplices to the Crime.*

N

Napoleonic Code. The code of laws adopted in France by the regime of Napoleon Bonaparte in 1810 and revised in 1819. The code became the basis for the criminal code in most continental European and Latin American countries. The basic premise is that individuals must prove their innocence in contrast to common law in which the burden of proof rests with the state.

narcissism. Is a term for self-love in a degree beyond self-esteem. The condition is named for Narcissus, a youth in Greek legend who fell in love with his reflection in a pool and pined away to death while admiring himself.

Freud distinguished earlier and later stages of narcissism. He considered *primary narcissism* normal in infants, who focus on their own bodies and gratify their pleasure drives by such activities as sucking and eating. If character development proceeds normally, children turn their pleasure-seeking drives to other people. However, if love objects are lost, an immature or disturbed person may develop *secondary narcissism* and revert to absorption with self.

narcissistic personality disorder. People with this disorder may display the following traits: grandiosity; need for admiration; boastful and pretentious; and interpersonally exploitative (may assume that they do not have to wait in line).

National Crime Victimization Survey (NCVS). The measurement of actual criminal victimization other than traditional reporting models (Uniform Crime Reports). NCVS was created in 1972 under the Bureau of the Census. The program conducts a national survey of households and individuals to approximate the amount of crime that occurs in the United States. Approximately 60,000 household interviews and 125,000 personal interviews are conducted biannually. Information is collected on each household member who is 12 years of age or older. Anyone within the household unit who is 14 years or older can be interviewed. Household members are categorized three ways: household respondents, self-respondents, and proxy respondents. Household respondents answer questions pertaining to everyone in the household. Self-respondents, who are at least 14 years of age, answer questions that relate directly to themselves. Proxy respondents provide data for household members aged 12 or 13, or for members not available for interviews. Data are collected on six of the eight UCR Part I offenses. As the survey is based on interviews of the victim, data on homicide are obviously not collected. The crime of arson is also excluded because it is often difficult to determine responsibility. Data involving business (NCVS) surveys was suspended in 1977. Also excluded were government office buildings, farms, and household "cottage" industries.

natural explanations. This approach is an attempt to explain the actions of mankind as both ancient and modern. The early Phoenicians and Greeks developed naturalistic explanations for behavior early in their history. Hippocrates (460 B.C.) provided a physiological explanation of thinking by arguing that the brain is the organ of the mind. Democritus (420 B.C.) suggested the idea of an indestructible unit of matter called the atom as central to his explanation of the world around him. With Socrates, Plato, and Aristotle, the concepts of unity and continuity became prominent, but the essential factors in all natural explanations were physical and material (*See*: spiritual).

natural law. The philosophical perspective that certain immutable rights are fundamental to human nature and can be readily ascertained through reason. Man-made laws, in contrast, are said to derive from human experience and history—both of which are subject to continual change.

natural rights. The rights that, according to natural law theorists, individuals retain in the face of government action, regulation, and interests.

neoclassical school. A trend in the history of criminology that flourished in Europe during the early 19th century. It modified the views of the classical school of criminology by introducing the concepts of diminished criminal responsibility and less severe punishment due to the age or mental condition of the offender.

neo-Lombrosians. Contemporary criminologists who emphasize psychopathological states as causes of crime.

net-widening. Also referred to as widening the net. Applies to situations where the intended goal is to improve efficiency and reduce criminal justice control over low risk offenders but where in fact the consequence is to expand control. For example, diversion programs are meant to "divert" offenders out of the criminal justice system in order to avoid the stigma of conviction and to reduce court calendars. These offenders often fail to complete the diversion programs and are referred back to court for prosecution, often resulting in jail sentences. Prior to the availability of diversion programs, many or most of these cases would not have been prosecuted or such cases may have led to dismissals due to a lack of evidence. Alternative sentencing options, such as house arrest, electronic monitoring, and community service also serve to bring more individuals under the control of the criminal justice system without actual confinement.

neuroticism. A personality disorder marked by low self-esteem, excessive anxiety, and wide mood swings.

Niederhoffer, Arthur (1917-1981). Niederhoffer entered Brooklyn College at age 15 and graduated in 1937. He entered Brooklyn Law School earning his LL.B (converted to J.D. cum laude). In 1940, the same year of his New York State Bar admission, he joined the New York City Police Department. He was appointed sergeant in 1951 and lieutenant in 1956. He also earned a M.S. in Sociology in 1956 from Brooklyn College. His co-authored first book, *The Gang; A Study of Adolescent Behavior* was published in 1958. He continued his studies at New York University's Graduate School of Arts and Science and obtained his Ph.D. in 1963, two years after his retirement from the police department. During the final period of his 21-year police career, Niederhoffer instructed, supervised and trained recruits at the NY City Police Academy. Drawing from his doctoral dissertation "The Mobile Force: A Study of Police Cynicism" he devised a cynicism scale which has been widely replicated and measures cynicism in urban police departments and other occupations. After teaching at several institutions of higher learning, in 1967 he accepted a permanent position as a professor of sociology at John Jay College of Criminal Justice. He was awarded the college's presidential medal. That same year (1967) his book *Behind the Shield: The Police in Urban Society* was published. In *Behind the Shield,* Niederhoffer delineated a psychological and sociological profile of urban police officers and the social and organizational forces that mold their collective personality. In *The Ambivalent Force: Perspectives on the Police* (1970), co-authored with Abraham S. Blumberg, they examined the ambiguities of the police role. In 1974, Niederhoffer and Smith wrote *New Directions in Police-Community Relations*, a book that offered a practical guide to police-community relations, using case studies, questionnaires, and interviews. He and his wife, Elaine, in 1978 published *The Police Family: From Station House to Ranch House,* which was a behind-the-scenes look at police-oriented family life. In 1980, he was elected a fellow of the American Society of Criminology.

nonintervention. A principle often associated with labeling theory, which concludes that the least amount of encroachment by the criminal justice system into a persons life, the better his or her chances of conforming to societal standards. In other words, the less involvement, the better (*See*: Becker, Howard; labeling theory).

nonparticipant observation. A study in which investigators observe closely but do not be come participants.

norms. Shared values that delineate the conduct suitable in a given circumstance.

nurturant strategy. A crime control model that attempts to forestall development of criminality by improving early life experiences and channeling child and adolescent development into socially desirable directions.

O

obsessive-compulsive personality disorder. Behavior patterns include: preoccupation with orderliness, perfectionism; excessively conscientious; scrupulous; mercilessly self-critical; and rigidly deferential to authority.

occupational crime. Any act punishable by law that is committed through opportunity created in the course of an occupation that is legal.

operant behavior. Behavior that affects the environment in such a way as to produce responses or further behavioral cues. Behavior that is strengthened or weakened by the consequences which follow.

operant conditioning. Associated with social learning theory, which holds that behavior is shaped by the consequences that follow it. When behavior is followed by positive reinforcement or reward the probability that the behavior will be repeated is increased. When behavior is followed by punishment, the probability that the behavior will be repeated is decreased or diminished (*See*: Pavlov, Ivan).

opportunity structure. A path to achieve goals. Opportunity structures may be of two types: legal (legitimate) and illegal (illegitimate).

oppositional defiant disorder. A pattern of negativistic, defiant, disobedient and hostile behavior toward authority figures.

Order of Misericordia. This group was founded in 1488 to provide assistance and consolation to offenders condemned to death. Members accompanied prisoners to the gallows, furnished religious services, and provided a Christian burial.

order maintenance. The "non-law enforcement" activities of the police that serve to create and maintain social order and control. Activities such as intervening in domestic and neighborhood disturbances and conflicts.

Orwellian. A term derived from the name of George Orwell, the author of the novel 1984 that described a society totally controlled by an oppressive government.

overcriminalization. The overuse of the criminal law; making too many behaviors illegal; attempting to prevent or control particular behaviors with an over-reliance on sanctions.

P

parens patriae. A Latin term meaning "father of the fatherland." This is the assumption by the state of the role of guardian over children whose parents are deemed incapable or unfit.

Panopticon. A prison designed by Jeremy Bentham which was to be a circular building with cells along the circumference, each clearly visible from a central location staffed by guards.

paranoia. A psychiatric term designating a characteristic combination of mental symptoms, seen in many different types of mental and emotional disorders. There are two essential elements in reactions termed paranoid: (1) unrealistic feelings of self-overevaluation, grandeur, or grandiosity; and (2) unrealistic and irrational beliefs of being persecuted. The word paranoia is derived from two Greek roots: *para*, which means beside, and *nous*, meaning intellect or reason. The term thus implies a "mind beside itself."

paranoid schizophrenics. Schizophrenic individuals who suffer from delusions and hallucinations.

Park, Robert Ezra (1864-1944). One of the developers of the "Chicago School," in which theorists focused on the functions of social institutions and their breakdown. Crime was closely tied to particular neighborhoods and the conditions of the community. Some neighborhoods form "natural areas" of affluence or poverty. Different types of criminal conduct are associated with different areas. The Chicago School studied suburban "concentric zones" adjacent to Chicago. They considered areas of urban renewal as "interstitial areas" or areas in transition. In developing this theory, Robert Park collaborated with Edwin Sutherland, Louis Wirth, and Ernest W. Burgess.

parole. The conditional release of an offender from prison under supervision after that individual has served a portion of his or her sentence. Under indeterminate sentencing statutes, an inmate was generally eligible for parole after completion of one-third of the original sentence. Under determinate sentencing statutes, offenders must generally serve a significant portion of their sentence before release (*See:* Spears, Charles).

participant observation. The collection of information and data through active involvement in the social life of the group a researcher is studying.

participatory justice. A relatively informal type of criminal justice case processing that makes use of local community resources rather than requiring traditional forms of official intervention.

Pavlov, Ivan P. (1849-1936). A Russian neurphysiologist associated with conditioned learning theories. He conducted experiments in the process of learning the late 1880s. Pavlov conditioned his experimental dogs to the sound of a bell. Initially, the dogs would salivate when they saw and smelled food. Pavlov rang the bell immediately after each feeding. After repeating this process several times, the dogs would begin to salivate at the sound of the bell without seeing or smelling food. The reflexes controlling the salivary glands became conditioned to anticipate a rewarding consequence (food) at the sound of the bell.

peace model. An approach to crime control that focuses on effective ways for developing a shared consensus on critical issues which have the potential to seriously affect the quality of life.

peacemaking criminology. A perspective which holds that crime-control agencies and citizens they serve should work together to alleviate social problems and human suffering and thus reduce crime.

Peel, Sir Robert (1788-1850). Born in Bury, Lancashire, England, and educated at Oxford. In 1812, Peel accepted the post of chief secretary for Ireland and, during his term of office, made his reputation as an able and incorruptible administrator. He sought passage of the Peace Preservation Act of 1814, which made possible the formation of a body of national police, later to become known as the Royal Irish Constabulary, popularly called The Peelers.

In 1822, he accepted a seat in the cabinet of Parliament. As the British Home Secretary in 1829, Peel introduced into Parliament an act for improving the police in and near London. He believed that a community needed a protective body of well-selected and trained men in order to prevent crime and institute social control. He reformed criminal laws by limiting their scope and reducing unfair penalties. Peel removed the death penalty from more than 100 offenses. Most important, he established 12 fundamental principles of quality policing that are still applicable today.

penal couple. A term describing the relationship between victim and criminal. Also, the two individuals most involved in the criminal act—the offender and the victim.

Penn, William (1644-1718). An English Quaker who fought for religious freedom and individual rights. In 1681 he obtained a charter from King Charles II and founded the Quaker settlement of Pennsylvania. He served as Governor of Pennsylvania from 1682 to 1692. Penn is the author of penological reforms known as *The Great Law,* which substituted imprisonment at hard labor for the death penalty for a majority of serious crimes.

penologist. A social scientist who studies and applies the theory and methods of punishment for crime.

penology (Also called corrections). The study of various programs, social structures, and administrative organizations for the treatment and security of criminal offenders, along with the evaluation of the effectiveness of such efforts. Commonly referred to as institutional corrections.

persisters. Offenders who do not grow out of criminality and become career criminals *(See*: chronic offender; career criminal).

personality disorders. These are inflexible, and pervasive behavior patterns that are maladaptive. They are generally adopted early in life and continue through adulthood. The behavior exhibited usually resembles, in a milder, less serious form, the behavior of more serious disorders. For example, people diagnosed with compulsive personality disorder are, like those diagnosed with obsessive compulsive disorder, constricted in their actions, in relations with others, work, play, and so on. The difference is that the former is less severe and maladaptive and does not appear and then later remit as an illness typically does.

The concept of personality disorder is controversial because these disorders have not been widely researched, which means that relatively little is known about them, and because their diagnosis tends to be unreliable. (The major exception is antisocial personality.)

<u>Paranoid Personality Disorder.</u> Some of the following symptoms are present: suspicion and mistrust of others often characterized by hypervigilance, guardedness, doubt of loyalty of others, and preoccupation with special meanings and hidden motives. There is a marked hypersensitivity which results in feelings of being slighted, exaggeration of problems, inability to relax, and a willingness to attack when a real or imagined threat is perceived. Affectively, these people appear to be cool and unemotional. They lack a sense of humor and are unable to express warn, tender, sentimental feelings.

<u>Schizoid Personality Disorder.</u> Individuals with this disorder are emotionally cold and aloof. They seldom exhibit warm tender feelings. They appear indifferent to praise or criticism and to the feelings of others. Generally

there are only one or two close relationships with others, including family members.

Schizotypal Personality Disorder. This disorder involves oddities of thought, speech, perception, and behavior that are quite similar to schizophrenia but not serious enough to be given that diagnosis. The disorder may include paranoid ideations, ideas of reference, magical thinking, social isolation, a frequent sense of having others present even though they are not, and speech patterns that are vague and digressive but not incoherent. There may be periods of inappropriate response of emotion, often accompanied by suspicion and social anxiety.

Histrionic Personality Disorder. Also called *hysterical personality disorder*, this disorder is characterized by dramatic or reactive symptoms, including exaggerated emotion, attention-getting behavior, need for excitement, overreaction to minor events, and temper tantrums or angry outbursts. In addition the individual may be shallow and superficial, self-indulgent and inconsiderate, vain and demanding, or dependent. There are instances of suicidal threats, which are manipulative in nature.

Narcissistic Personality Disorder. This disorder is characterized by exaggerated self-importance with inflated descriptions of accomplishments. There are frequent fantasies centering around success, power, beauty, love, and intelligence. The individual requires constant attention and there are inappropriate expressions of rage, indifference, shame, etc. At least two of the following symptoms are present: (1) expectations of special favors; (2) interpersonal exploitation; (3) extremes of idealization or devaluation of relationships; and (4) almost complete lack of empathy with others.

Antisocial Personality Disorder. This disorder, more commonly known as *psychopathic* or *sociopathic* behavior, appears most in diagnoses of chronic law violators. It has an estimated incidence of three percent in men and one percent in women in the United States. Behavior shows consistent violation of the rights of others that begins before age 15 and continues into adult life. There is generally a failure to maintain a satisfactory employment record. Acts of lying, stealing, fighting, and truancy are childhood symptoms. These conditions remain and sometimes intensify during adolescence. In addition, adolescence usually brings sexual behavior problems, sometimes of an assaultive nature, and there is also an increase in abuse of substances such as alcohol and illicit drugs. These symptoms usually remain during early adulthood and tend to diminish somewhat around the age of 30. Generally speaking, this disorder causes an impairment in interpersonal relationships, with an inability to establish and maintain close relationships, socially or within the family. Characteristically, antisocial personalities tend not to show any remorse for their actions and not to learn from experience, including punishment for their criminal acts, which make treatment extremely difficult.

Borderline Personality Disorder. There is a basic instability in interpersonal relationships, mood, and self-concept. Relationships that are established tend to shift from intense to unstable. Impulsive and unpredictable behavior is common with unstable mood and in some cases there is identity disturbance centering around self-image or gender identity. It is not uncommon for a person to have other personality disorders in conjunction with the borderline personality disorder. This disorder seems to occur more often in females than in males.

Avoidant Personality Disorder. Persons with this disorder tend to be hypersensitive to possible rejection, shame, or humiliation. There is a marked reluctance to enter into relationships without guarantees of unconditional acceptance. This often results in social withdrawal despite the intense need for acceptance and affection. The consequences of this behavioral pattern are periods of anxiety, depression, and self hate.

Dependent Personality Disorder. The person with this disorder is extremely passive and permits others to make decisions for his or her life. This is due in part to an inability to function adequately alone and in part to an extreme lack of self-confidence. Persons with this disorder subordinate their own needs in favor of significant others.

Compulsive Personality Disorder. This disorder is characterized by a preoccupation with trivial details, rules, and efficiency, with the effect that the individual cannot see "the big picture" and behaves rigidly, with no spontaneity. People displaying this disorder are stingy with their emotions and material items so that, for example, interpersonal relations tend to be stiff and formal. They also value work and productivity and have a difficult time relaxing; leisure activities are overly planned and structured so as to rob them of their enjoyment. Decision-making is avoided, perhaps for fear of making a mistake.

Passive-Aggressive Personality Disorder. Individuals with this disorder meet the demands of their environment by resisting indirectly. For example, rather than refuse to perform a task, the person will procrastinate until the deadline is passed or will perform the task poorly. In both instances the person is assumed to be passively expressing aggressive feelings, which is the origin of the disorder's name. Obviously there is both social and occupational impairment.

Atypical, Mixed, or other Personality Disorder. This diagnosis is used for those people who meet the diagnostic criteria for more than one personality disorder or for those people who meet the criteria of a personality disorder but not of a specific type.

personality tests. Instruments used in an effort to predict behavior. In criminology, personality tests are used in an attempt to predict deviant or antisocial behavior. Personality tests tend to be of two types. The first type, projective tests like the Rorschach Inkblot Test and the Thematic Apperception Test are administered by clinicians who then interpret responses. The second and more commonly used tests are personality inventories. The personality inventory is generally a test given to a person who is asked to agree or disagree with a series of questions. The most widely-used personal inventory is the Minnesota Multiphasic Personality Inventory (MMPI), which has a number of scales that measure levels of psychopathic deviation, schizophrenia, and hypomania (*See*: Minnesota Multiphasic Personality Inventory).

pharmacology. The branch of science that deals with the study of drugs and their effects of living systems.

phenomenological criminology. Views crime as a concept created through a process of social interaction, and details the existence of criminal reality via exploration of the world view of mindset characteristics of committed career offenders.

phenomenology. The study of the contents of human consciousness without regard to external conventions or prior assumptions.

Philadelphia Birth Cohort Study. A 1972 study by Marvin Wolfgang and his associates that significantly influenced the concept of the chronic offender. In this study Wolfgang followed the criminal careers of a cohort of 9,945 boys born in Philadelphia in 1945. The most notable finding had to do with the chronic offender or career criminal. Wolfgang and his associates were able to identify 627 boys out of this sample that had been arrested five times or more. These chronic offenders, as they were called, represented 6 percent of the total sample of 9,945 and were involved in the greatest number of delinquent acts. This chronic 6 percent were responsible for 5,305 crimes, or approximately 42 percent of all offenses. Wolfgang found that arrest and criminal justice system processing did little to deter this group of offenders. (*See:* Wolfgang, Marvin)

Philadelphia plan (Pennsylvania system). The organizing principle for prisons developed by the Quakers in the early 19th century. It was based on the assumption that the criminal was a sinner and in need of repentance. Hence, prisoners were put in solitary confinement with the Bible to reflect on their crimes.

They were required to read or work in solitude and silence. This system competed with the New York, or congregate system, that allowed inmates to work with other inmates but still in silence. The Philadelphia plan tended to result in a high rate of mental problems, suicide, and deteriorated health. Due to these problems the New York plan eventually won over the Philadelphia system.

philosophy. A term derived from a Greek word meaning "love of wisdom." Ancient Greeks called philosophers sought wisdom in all fields—the structure of matter, the nature of the good, the reality of God. In modern times scholars specialize—physicists conduct experiments to identify the particles of matter, theologians study about religion and God, philosophers still ponder about questions such as "What is god?" The range of interests still pursued by philosophers can be shown by listing major fields: metaphysics, the study of the first principles of reality; epistemology, the theory of knowledge; logic, the principles of inductive and deductive reasoning; ethics, the study of right and wrong; aesthetics, the study of what is beautiful. Historically, philosophy evolved from the classical, or the Greek and Roman period characterized by a quest for the meaning of reality as exemplified in the philosophies of Socrates, Plato, Aristotle, and Plotinus. Early Christian thought, or medieval philosophy, explored the relationship between faith and reason under such teachers as St. Augustine and Thomas Aquinas. By the Renaissance period, modern philosophy began to take shape. Philosophers, such as Rene Descartes, Baruch Spinoza, John Locke, Immanuel Kant, Georg Hegel, John Stuart Mill, and Bertrand Russell, applied science to philosophy.

phrenology. A theory of personality and method of studying its traits that was very popular in the first half of the 19th century but is now considered pseudoscience. Phrenologists believed that personality could be divided into a number of specific traits and that each of these faculties was centered in a particular region of the brain. Maps of the head were drawn to show the location of faculties, and bumps on the skull were taken as evidence of strong development of the corresponding characteristic. One aspect of phrenology was the study of personality traits to explain the combative, aggressive, and criminal behavior. The first phrenology book, *The Outlines of Phrenology,* was written in 1832 by Johann Kasper Spurzheim, M.D., of the universities of Vienna and Paris and a licentiate of the Royal College of Physicians of London.

physiognomy. The belief that personality traits can be judged from physical appearance, particularly the form and expression of the face. An Italian criminologist, Cesare Lombroso claimed he could identify criminal types of people by "degenerate" characteristics such as low brows and eyes set too close together. His ideas had considerable popularity in the first part of the 20th century, but they have since been rejected by scientists. (*See:* Lavater, Johan; Lombroso, Cesare)

picaresque organizations. A relatively permanent gang under the leadership of a single person who sometimes relies on the support and advice of a few officers.

Plato (427-347 B.C.). A philosopher of ancient Greece. Spending eight years as Socrates' disciple, Plato was one of the most influential thinkers in the history of Western civilization. He founded his Academy of philosophy near Athens in 387, and taught there until his death. His works are well-preserved, including more than 25 dialogues and some letters. In the *Republic*, one of his most important works, he argued that the operation of justice cannot be fully understood unless seen in relation to the idea of the good, which is the supreme principle of order and truth. Throughout his writings, Plato touched on almost every problem that has occupied subsequent philosophers (*See:* philosophy).

pluralistic ignorance. A situation in which witnesses in a group fail to help the victim of an emergency or a crime because they interpret the failure of other witnesses to assist as a sign that no help is necessary.

pluralistic perspective. An analytical approach to social organization, which holds that a multiplicity of values and beliefs exist in any complex society, but that most social actors agree on the usefulness of law as a formal means of dispute resolution.

political criminology. The criminological study of politics, which, in turn, involves the regulation and control of the citizenry. *Power* is central to the concept of political criminology. It refers to the ability of one to control another.

The most extreme form of the theory of political crime is that all crime is political, because acts are made criminal offenses to protect the interests, values, and beliefs of the lawmaking class. A less radical view is that ordinary crimes attack a small part of the society's value system, while political crimes strike at the whole value system or its leading institutions. Political crimes are those acts perceived as a direct threat to the established political power, with the political criminal acting on behalf of a conflicting system. Certain actions, such as protests against the Vietnam War or the Civil Rights movement were, at that time, perceived by many as political crimes.

popular justice. Attempts by local neighborhoods and communities to devise informal and non-bureaucratic alternatives to the official justice system (e.g., unofficial neighborhood or community courts and police patrols).

positivism. The application of scientific techniques to the study of crime and criminals. Also referred to as deterministic explanations using a variety of perspectives including biological, sociological, and psychological.

post-crime victimization or **secondary victimization.** A term referring to problems in living that tend to follow from initial victimization.

positive school of criminal law. This is a term applied to legal scholars who, in the latter half of the 19th century, urged the reform of the criminal law in the light of scientific discoveries concerning the causes of criminal conduct. The impetus was derived from French philosopher August Comte's (1798-1857) positivism on the one hand, and the research of criminal anthropologists on the other. Its leading proponent was the Italian scholar Enrico Ferri, and it greatly influenced criminal law reform, particularly on the continent. *(See* Ferri, Enrico)

post-modern criminology. A brand of criminology that developed following World War II, and which builds upon the tenents inherent in postmodern social thought.

Pound, Roscoe (1870-1964). An educator and legal scholar, born in Lincoln, Neb. He taught law at the University of Nebraska from 1899 to 1903, was dean of the law department from 1903 to 1907, and was a legal adviser to the state government from 1904 to 1907, holding the post of commissioner of uniform state laws. In 1907, he joined the law faculty at Northwestern, taught law at the University of Chicago from 1909 to 1910, and then joined the Harvard law faculty; he was dean of the Harvard Law School from 1916 to 1936. During his later years, he shared with Learned Hand the reputation of being the nation's leading jurist outside of the Supreme Court bench.

poverty, culture of. The idea of a "culture of poverty" was developed in the 1960s by Oscar Lewis and other social scientists. They believed that poverty-stricken people anywhere in the world share certain values, beliefs, and attitudes toward the world. The poor are generally fatalistic about their lives, ill at ease in middle-class institutions, present-oriented, hedonistic, have low self-esteem, and live lives that are often intertwined with violence in their own families or neighborhoods. As a result, they are cynical about getting ahead in the world. The culture of poverty stresses "knowing the right person" or "being lucky" rather than hard work to advance socially. Edward C. Banfield, in *Unheavenly City* and his subsequent work *Unheavenly City Revisited,* explores this concept of culture in relation to urban problems and crime.

Some social scientists assumed that the best way to put an end to poverty is to change the values of the poor. This view has been severely criticized by those who maintain that advanced capitalism destroys job opportunities for the poor through automation and that less mechanized industries, such as corporate fruit-growing, need a poor class of people to draw on for cheap labor. One question, then, becomes, Is poverty maintained by the fatalistic values of the poor themselves or by an economic system that promotes poverty by its unconcern for human values? Another position suggests that the welfare system in the United States has created a culture of poverty that has been passed through generations. A further position is that the large majority of inmates in county jails and state prisons are from lower and working classes. Thus, the prison industry not only prospers through lower-class populations but obliquely serves to "protect society."

power-control theory. A perspective which holds that the distribution of crime and delinquency within society is to some degree founded upon the consequences which power relationships within the wider society hold for domestic settings, and for the everyday relationships between men, women, and children within the context of family life.

pragmatism. A philosophical view generally credited to William James and John Dewey that stresses that concepts should be analyzed and evaluated in terms of practical consequences. In this view, actions designed to achieve desired goals are appropriate by reason of that fact and need have no theoretical rationale.

praxis. This simply means the application of a theory to action or practice. In Marxist criminology, the term is used to explain the cause(s) of revolution.

predatory crime. Individual property crimes such as theft, burglary, and larceny that are committed primarily for the sake of the perpetrator's survival.

prejudice. A negative, irrational and inflexible attitude toward a concept or group of people.

preponderence of evidence. The burden of proof required in a civil proceeding. A lesser weight of evidence than "beyond a reasonable doubt" which is the standard required in a criminal proceeding. For example, O.J. Simpson was acquitted in his criminal trial when a jury could not find him guilty beyond a reasonable doubt. However, a civil jury later found him liable for the two murders when using the lesser burden of proof. The proponderence of evidence is also the standard required at a probation or parole violation proceeding.

pressure groups. These consist of any group having a distinct ideology or set of goals and attempting to achieve those goals through the use of organized means of interaction, such as lobbying. Pressure groups may be distinguished from the broader category of *interest groups* by their somewhat more formal organization and their more noticeable activity over time. The United States political system has always been composed, in part, of such pressure groups, and much legislation and policy are made only after consideration of the desires of such groups has taken place. Pressure groups may be seen as representing both the strongest and the weakest features of American politics. Two major pressure groups are the National Rifle Association and the International Association of Chiefs of Police.

prevalence. The proportion of a population that commits crime over a given period of time. It is measured by the number of offenders divided by the size of the population.

preventive detention. The authority of the court to order a defendant held in custody without bail after a finding is made that he or she poses a danger to the community if released. Also may be ordered if it is found that the accused is likely to flee the jurisdiction of the court.

prima facie case. A case in which there is as much evidence as would warrant the conviction of the defendant if properly proved in court, unless contradicted; a case that meets evidentiary requirements for grand-jury indictment.

primary deviance. Initial deviance often undertaken to deal with transient problems in living.

primary groups. More correctly termed *small groups*, primary groups were first studied and distinguished by William James, Charles Horton Cooley, and George Herbert Mead to determine their effects on personality development. Many contemporary social and behavioral scientists view these groups as having a certain permanence, which is provided by a relatively small membership holding a wide variety of common interests and valuing face-to-face communication. These "natural" groups are the family, one's social group, the work group, and the neighborhood.

principals. Perpetrators of a criminal act.

prisons (penitentiary). In the modern sense prisons are a relatively recent development in the history of mankind. Until the reforms growing out of the 18th-century Enlightenment, those convicted of crime were more often fined, banished, publicly whipped, or executed than locked up. And although colonial jails were established in Massachusetts and Pennsylvania in the 17th century, they hardly resembled the institutions that the term "prison" implies today. In fact, during the colonial and early national period of American history, such places of confinement were solely for detention and made no pretense of rehabilitation. Inmates in modern prisons have been convicted of a felony and sentenced to a period in excess of one year.

19th-Century Developments. Prisons as they are now known in America and Europe had their beginning in the early 19th century. They were intended to stress reform instead of punishments and to correct the evil conditions and idleness that characterized the jails. The concern of the reformers led to the development of two different types of prisons in New York and Pennsylvania. Both systems built massive structures to house convicted criminals and sought to reform them through "hard labor in solitary confinement" into temperate, hard-working citizens. It was no accident that the first prison in Pennsylvania was called a "penitentiary," for the prisoner was kept in complete isolation so that, alone with his Bible and work, he could do penance.

Auburn Prison in New York opened in 1819. Here prisoners lived in separate cells, but they worked in groups. Both the New York and Pennsylvania prisons separated prisoners for discipline and to avoid contamination of one another, and both emphasized work. It was assumed that idleness had led to the corruption of the inmates.

Reformers came from various European countries to observe the Auburn and Pennsylvania prisons. One of these observers was Alexis de Tocqueville, who referred to the pervasive effect of the rule of silence at Auburn prison "as a desert solitude."

European prisons developed largely after the Pennsylvania model, but for economic reasons most American prisons in the 19th century were patterned on the Auburn model. These early prisons were involuntary factories as well as bleak penitentiaries and often made a profit. As more Auburn-like prisons were built, however, they evoked criticism by reformers in the 1870s, the "golden age of penal reform." In this decade the National Prison Association was founded, one of its principles being that "reformation, not vindictive suffering" should be the purpose of prisons. At the first meeting of this association in Cincinnati, "The Declaration of Principles" was adopted. These principles were so advanced that they were reiterated nearly a hundred years later by the President's Commission on Law Enforcement and the Administration of Justice (1967).

These advances in theory were not followed in practice, although New York made an effort to do so in its Elmira Reformatory, which was opened in 1867. Its architecture was patterned after the fortress-like structure of Auburn, however, and it soon became another walled prison, though its inmates were younger. One lasting reform was parole, which was first instituted in this country at Elmira. Elmira's educational program was to have been its main focus, but it did not become viable until the 1930s.

20th-Century Reforms and Problems. Prison reform received renewed impetus in the 1930s, when the federal prison system demonstrated that effective programs of rehabilitation could be established if qualified personnel were recruited. The Federal Bureau of Prisons still seeks to lead, and even prod, the various state systems in architectural planning as well as in program development. The Depression curtailed this progress. However, better-educated personnel, who would not have considered such employment in ordinary times, were recruited.

The era after World War II brought both reforms and a wave of riots. Changes in California were so notable that American prisons once again served as models for Europeans. The riots of the 1950s were widely publicized, but as in the 1970s, attention was focused on the symptoms more often that on basic causes. The American Prison Association's report focused on one basic problem highlighted by the uprising at Attica State Prison in New York in 1971—the deeply felt injustice of unwise sentencing and parole practices." Rehabilitation, the cornerstone of liberal penal philosophy, fell by the wayside. Today, confinement is considered punishment. Toward that end, on May 10, 1995, the Limestone Prison facility in Alabama became the first American prison to institute chain gangs in more than 30 years. Prisoners are shackled at the ankle with three-pound leg irons and bound together by eight-foot lengths of chain. Other states, believing that prisoners "have it too easy," have enacted legislation to remove or restrict the inmate use of weights, television and other creature comforts.

Many contemporary observers feel that the single greatest prison problem is overcrowding. In 1994, approximately 38 states were under federal mandates limiting prison populations.

Prisoners, over the years, have filed lawsuits challenging the administration of prisons, over disciplinary actions and violations of due process. In 1993, more than 33,000 lawsuits were filed by state inmates in federal courts, a fivefold increase since 1977. On June 19, 1995, a U.S. Supreme Court decision restricted inmate complaints over disciplinary measures, such as solitary confinement. This case (*Sandin vs. Conner*, 93-1911) could curb the amount of future claims.

Prison Populations. There are 53 jurisdictions having prison populations, the 50 states and the federal government (U.S. Bureau of Prisons), the District of Columbia and Puerto Rico. Within the 50 States the various counties maintain a separate jail system (sentences usually less than one year). Each county and state also has a juvenile justice system. The prison population of the states exceeded 1 million during 1995, while the federal prisoner count was at 125,000. The county jails hold approximately 400,000 (Los Angeles County alone has a continuing inmate population exceeding 20,000).

prisonization. The more direct, negative effects of imprisonment—adopting, to a greater or lesser degree, the values, orientation, and life-style of the prison subculture.

private justice. The sale of policing and correctional services, of "justice, safety, and protection," by private, operated-for-profit security firms and treatment and rehabilitative agencies.

probation. The conditional freedom granted by a judicial officer to an alleged or adjudged adult or juvenile offender, as long as the person meets certain conditions of behavior.

Probation has its antecedents in the common law phenomenon of suspended sentence. The first probation system in the world without restriction as to age was legally established as a judicial policy by Boston, Mass, in 1878 and throughout Mass. in 1880. This form of judicial disposition was subsequently utilized by all states by 1957.

probation officer. The person responsible for the preparation of the presentence investigation report (PSI) and the supervision of offenders placed on probation by the court.

problem behavior syndrome (PBS). A position that suggests a clustering of antisocial behaviors involving hedonistic pleasures, such as substance abuse, smoking, precocious sexual behavior and early pregnancy, as well as educational and other areas of underachievement, suicide attempts, and thrill-seeking are in combination precursors to criminality.

problem-oriented policing. A strategy to enhance community relations and to improve crime prevention whereby police work with citizens to identify and respond to problems in a given community.

professional crime. This is defined as regular participation in criminal activity that involves a complex array of skills and relies on a system of status and organization of a specialized nature. Professional crime involves offenses against property as opposed to crimes against a person. Fraud, banking schemes, and computer crime fall under this category.

professionalization. Although there is a variety of specific definitions for this term, there is some agreement that the process by which an occupation comes to be defined as a profession involves the specification of a body of knowledge or theory that defines an area of expertise, the emergence of professional associations and, concomitantly, an increase in group identity, specialized training, extensive educational requirements, scholarly publications, social acceptance, the formulation of codes of appropriate behavior, and the development of a sense of commitment or obligation to a clientele. The three traditional professions are: theology, law and medicine.

progressive system. In penology, a prison program patterned after the Irish system. According to this system, instituted by Sir Walter Crofton, a prisoner advanced progressively from initial cell isolation and lack of privileges to congregate life with increasing privileges. Such advancement into a new grade or class was earned by acquiring credits for good behavior, industry, and interest in education. The later phases of progressive advancement were designed to include minimum custody in an intermediate prison, where self-control could be fostered and the prisoner prepared for the discharge by parole. The system is sometimes called the graded system. It has never been completely followed, but many modern prison systems have incorporated aspects and general principles of the system, especially the earning of privileges, promotions to jobs of trust, and classification for degree of custody, such as close, medium, and minimum. In general, inmates in prison systems that have used the principles embodied in the Irish system do not pass through all the stages of custody. Instead, they are classified at admission regarding the degree of custody required, but can be reclassified upward or downward in custodial level as time and circumstances warrant. (*See*: Crofton)

proletariat. In Marxist theory, the working class.

protection/avoidance strategy. A crime control strategy that attempts to reduce criminal opportunities by changing people's routine activities or by incapacitating convicted offenders via incarceration or electronic monitoring devices.

Protestant ethic. Max Weber observed in *The Protestant Ethic* and the *Spirit of Capitalism* (1904-1905) that historically, business and economic leaders, skilled labor and trained personnel, and owners of capital in centers of capitalist development were overwhelmingly Protestant. He found the explanation in the Calvinistic doctrine of predestination, according to which man is either saved or condemned eternally by God. Hard work could allay anxiety in this regard, and individual economic success could be construed as a sign of election for ultimate redemption. The income from hard work was not to be used for self-indulgence, so the righteous individual lived frugally, accumulating savings as sources of investment funds.

psychiatric theories. These theories derive from the medical sciences, including neurology, which, like other psychological theories, focuses on the individual as the unit of analysis.

psychoanalysis. An approach to clinical treatment of individuals with neurotic tendencies that is based on the work of Austrian psychiatrist Sigmund Freud, who believed that many sexual desires are subconsciously repressed in early life and must be identified and understood by patients through such methods as free association and dream analysis. The classic psychoanalytic method included frequent, often daily, appointments with a therapist and the use of a couch, but these traditions have been modified and adapted by many later theories of psychiatric illness and its treatment.

According to Freud, most problems experienced in adulthood can be traced to traumatic events that occurred in childhood.

psychoanalytic criminology. A psychiatric approach developed by Sigmund Freud that emphasized the role of personality in human behavior, and which sees deviant behavior as the result of dysfunctional personalities. Problems leading to criminal behavior are often located deep in the unconscious mind.

psychodiagnosis. A method of diagnosis used in investigating the origin and cause of many emotional illnesses by examining a patient's mental condition. The diagnosis involves psychological tests and an investigation of the patient's past history as it relates to his or her psychiatric condition.

psychodrama. A method of psychotherapy in which patients play roles to act out troublesome situations. The enactment may be done on a stage, with professionals and other patients as the audience; the patient takes the leading role, staff or other patients play supporting roles, and the therapist is the director. The technique was developed early in the 20th century by American psychiatrist, Dr. J. L. Moreno.

psychological dependence. A compulsion to use a drug for its pleasurable or comforting effects. Such dependence may lead to physical addiction to the drug. A person may come to rely on drugs or alcohol to function despite the lack of a physical need.

psychological profiling. The attempt to categorize, understand, and predict, the behavior of certain types of offenders based upon behavioral clues they provide.

psychological theories. Are those theories derived from the behavioral sciences and that focus on the cognitive processes of the individual as the unit of analysis. Psychological theories place the locus of crime causation within the personality of the individual offender.

psychology. The science of behavior and cognition.

psychopath (sociopath). A person who is not psychotic but who has a severe personality disorder. The psychopath is deficient in the capacity to feel guilt, shame, or remorse; many engage in criminal behavior (*See*: anti-social personality).

psychopathology. The study of pathological or diseased mental conditions. The study of mental illness.

psychosis. Refers to a group of more than one mental disorder, drastic in nature, that interfere with organization of the personality and social relationships. Patients occasionally or frequently lose touch with reality, show inadequate self-control, and may engage in bizarre behavior. A psychotic condition may or may not be related to an organic disease and may be temporary or lifelong.

psychotherapy. Any of the wide variety of methods of treating psychological problems through a trained therapist's talking with a patient. Psychotherapy is distinguished from advice given and support offered by friends and family in that it is directed by a therapist with special training and a systematic approach. It is also often distinguished from behavior modification, a method of treatment that emphasizes learning to deal with troublesome situations by practicing certain behaviors rather than by talking about underlying feelings.

Psychotherapy is generally concerned with developing insight as a means of changing behavior, while behavior therapy strives to correct the troublesome behavior without dwelling on patient insight.

psychotic disorders. Generally considered the most severe of all mental disorders. While many psychotic conditions appear to be psychological reactions to various forms of stress, others are apparently caused by congenital organic or physical factors. The dominant characteristics of psychosis are personality disorganization and an impaired ability to perceive reality. The most common psychotic illness is schizophrenia (*See*: psychosis).

psychoticism. A dimension of the human personality describing individuals who are aggressive, egocentric, and impulsive.

punishment. The consequences of undesirable behavior. Increased sanctions are apt to decrease the frequency of the prohibited act or behavior which becomes the goal of deterrence theories. Any of a range of penalties imposed by a court after conviction of a criminal offense. These can include probation, probation with special conditions, and incarceration (*See*: criminal sanctions).

pyromania. Usually referred to as pathological fire setting, pyromania is a compulsion to start fires. This disorder has been called an obsessive-compulsive reaction or a symptom of an antisocial personality. The unconscious motivation for pyromania may be defiance of a particular authority figure or of society in general, a more general expression of aggression, or of sexual drives that do not find another outlet. Some compulsive arsonists watch the fires they start and become sexually aroused to the point of orgasm.

R

race. Divisions or groupings of humans by biological traits that have evolved as common to its members.

radical criminology. A contemporary school of criminology that focuses on the political nature of crime and criminal law and emphasizes repressive functions of government, governmental institutions and specifically, the criminal justice system. This is a perspective that holds that the causes of crime are rooted in economic conditions which empower the wealthy and the politically well-organized, but disenfranchise those less fortunate (*See:* conservative and liberal criminology; Marxist theory)

random sample. A sample selected in such a way as to ensure that each person in the population to be studied has an equal chance of being selected (*See:* sample).

rape. The unlawful sexual intercourse with a female, by force or without legal or factual consent.

rational choice theory. A classical criminological perspective that takes the position that crime and delinquency are the result of conscious free will and choice wherein the person weighs potential benefits against the potential consequences or punishment before acting. A matter of choice. Because this theory views the individual as weighing consequences, it necessarily views people as rational beings. (*See*: Beccaria, Cesare; routine activities theory; situational choice theory; Ehrlich's "Magic Bullet theory"; classical theory).

Ray, Isaac (1807-1881). Considered the most influential American writer on forensic psychiatry during the 19th century, Ray's chief lifetime interest was in the closer application of the law and psychiatry. He is primarily remembered as the author of *The Medical Jurisprudence of Insanity*, which first appeared in 1838 and dealt with the legal aspects of insanity. Ray held that insane persons should not be held responsible for criminal acts unless such acts could be proven not to be the direct or indirect result of insanity.

reaction formation. A defense mechanism developed by Sigmund Freud used to describe a manner of coping by behaving exactly opposite of how one actually feels. For example, a person may feel inferior but behave as if they are superior.

reaction subculture. A deviant delinquent subculture. Negative behavior is formed in reaction to the socially induced stresses that any social class system inflicts on the lower-class juveniles, among whom delinquency is concentrated. The concept is associated with criminologist Albert Cohen, author of the 1955 book *Delinquent Boys.*

realist criminology. An emerging perspective that insists upon a pragmatic assessment of crime and associated social problems.

reality therapy. William Glaser developed and tested reality therapy at the Ventura School for Girls in California. Reality therapy forces individuals to accept responsibility for their actions. The delinquent or public offender must face the consequences of the offense(s). Glaser holds that psychotherapy allows offenders to excuse or explain their deviant behavior, while reality therapy forces them to face and come to grips with their behavior.

rebellion. A mode of adaptation in which individuals reject cultural goals and develop a new set of goals, and reject institutionalized means to reach those goals and develop alternative sets of means; behavior in which a person seeks to create a new social structure that will more effectively allow people to meet goals that the rebel perceives to be appropriate (*See:* Merton, Robert).

recidivism. The repetition of criminal behavior. The goal of all correctional strategies is to reduce recidivism.

recidivism rate. The percentage of convicted offenders who have been released from prison and who are later rearrested for a new crime, generally within five years following release.

reformatory. A correctional facility originally intended as a place where youthful offenders could be "reformed." Many reformatories are now used for offenders regardless of age or offense, with the exception of capital crimes.

rehabilitation. To restore or return a person or thing to its former state or capacity. A widely accepted but seldom achieved goal of correctional agencies, generally relying on three basic elements: (1) individualization—emphasis on the offender, not the crime; (2) indeterminate sentencing structure—the release of the individual when cured rather than after a sentence has been served; (3) discretion—flexibility in managing the treatment of offenders.

reintegration. A philosophy of corrections that stresses the most positive method of reentry of the offender into the community. The goal is to establish or reestablish community ties with family, job, and friends.

reintegrative shaming. A process that follows expressions of community disapproval of an offender's behavior with gestures of reacceptance by the larger law-abiding community.

relative deprivation. The discrepancy between individuals' expectations about the goods and conditions of life to which they believe they are rightfully entitled, and their capabilities; or the goods and conditions of life they can attain and maintain under the current social and economic system.

resocialization. The process of learning and incorporating the rules and roles expected in a new setting because the old ones are no longer relevant.

restitution. A criminal sanction, in particular the payment of compensation by the offender to the victim.

restorative justice. A post-modern perspective that stresses remedies and restoration rather than prison, punishment and victim neglect.

retreatist subculture. A subculture whose members have abandoned the cultural goals and the socially approved means of achieving them. As an adaption to conflict, retreatism is characterized by the skid-row alcoholic, drug addicts, and the individual who resists the pressure to succeed by turning his or her back on material or other mainstream values.

retribution. A concept that implies the payment of a debt to society and thus the expiation of one's offense. It was codified in the biblical injunction, "an eye for an eye, a tooth for a tooth." A major goal of classical and just deserts theory holds that the punishment should be proportional to the seriousness of the crime.

revocation. The practice of withdrawing the privileges of probation or parole as a result of violating conditions and perhaps renegotiating the terms of probation or parole or reincarcerating the person.

robbery. The unlawful taking or attempted taking of property that is in the immediate possession of another, by force or threat of force.

Romilly, Sir Samuel (1757-1818). An English lawyer and law reformer who devoted his energies to changes in the harsh criminal codes. His efforts secured the repeal of many Elizabethan capital statutes and numerous other harsh and irrational laws. Along with John Howard, he sought to reform the infamous "bloody codes"—a system of laws that permitted execution for pickpocketing, cutting down trees on government parklands, setting fire to a cornfield, escaping from jail, and shooting a rabbit. Romilly also influenced the construction of the first modern English prison.

routine activities theory or **life-style theory.** A brand of rational choice theory which suggests that the activities or life-styles of victims often contribute to their victimization.

Rush, Benjamin (1745-1813). American psychiatrist, surgeon, and politician born in Philadelphia. He was a signer of the Declaration of Independence and regarded as the father of American psychiatry. He devoted much of his life to the reform of the treatment for the mentally ill, particularly at Pennsylvania Hospital. He recognized that insanity was a disease and that the patients should be treated rather than imprisoned, thereby bringing mental diseases into the area of medicine.

S

sadism. The desire to inflict pain, which may be either physical or psychological and is often associated with sexual behavior.

sadomasochism. A psychosexual disorder involving the inflicting of pain or suffering by one sexual partner (sadist) on the other, willing sexual partner (masochist) for the purposes of sexual arousal or gratification. In many sadomasochistic relationships, both partners willingly consent to their activities. The pain or suffering in such arrangements is generally not an end in itself and therefore usually remains minimal because the goal is sexual excitation rather than injury.

sample. A selected subset of a population to be studied (*See*: random sample).

scapegoating. This involves blaming another person or a group for one's own troubles, failures, or frustrations. Often minority groups become targets for displaced aggression.

schizophrenics. Those mentally ill individuals who suffer from disjointed thinking and, possibly, delusions and hallucinations. May include paranoia or feelings of persecution.

secondary deviance. A condition that generally results from official labeling and from association with others who have been so labeled.

segregation. Voluntary or involuntary, social or physical separation or exclusion of two or more individuals or groups of individuals.

selective incapacitation. A correctional policy which seeks to protect society by incarcerating those individuals deemed to be the most dangerous, including career or habitual offenders.

self-actualization. According to A. H. Maslow, this is the process of becoming all that one is capable of becoming, of developing a unique self motivated by an unselfish need for growth versus survival; according to G.H. Mead, the process of becoming a social and human being resulting from reflected self-appraisals from others—becoming self-conscious; in Buddhist philosophy, the process of integrating the self as to achieve oneness or unity; for the philosopher Immanuel Kant, achieving self-knowledge.

self-concept. This is the sum total of the perceptions, feelings, and beliefs that people have about themselves. The self-concept can be thought of as having two parts: one that includes characteristics and personality traits, (tall, conceited, intelligent, and so forth), the second that is an evaluation of the worth or desirability of the traits (self-esteem).

According to Charles H. Cooley and George H. Mead, individuals develop a self-concept by observing how others treat them. In early childhood parents and siblings are most influential in determining self-concept. Later the scope widens to include friends, teachers, and other influential people. Individuals also develop a self-concept by comparing themselves to others. Ideas about characteristics and worth are also strongly affected by the environment.

Theorists often differentiate between the traits or characteristics that are considered central to the self-concept and those that are not. Centrality refers both to the degree of importance that the individual attaches to that particular trait and to its degree of influence in determining behavior. An inconsistent self-concept is one in which the characteristics seem to contradict one another, as in a person who thinks he is both a left-wing radical and an advocate of traditional values.

Many methods of measuring self-concept have been developed. Among the most popular are questionnaires listing a number of adjectives or, in the case of self-esteem, statements of self-worth, each of which the respondent checks as being either true or false. Individuals have also been asked to write 15 or 20 responses to the question: Who am I?

self-fulfilling prophecy. This is the prediction of events that do, in fact, happen because the prediction becomes the cause.

Self-fulfilling prophecies are often causes of deviant behavior. Some criminologists believe that a person does not become deviant until labeled so by the authorities. Likewise, educational performances may reflect the expectations and fulfilling prophecies of teachers. In many experimental studies the theories of the experiments tend to be "proved," even when different theories make opposite predictions. (*See:* labeling theory).

self-report surveys. A survey in which respondents answer in a confidential interview or, most often, by completing an anonymous questionnaire (*See:* drug abuse surveys).

sentence. The punishment imposed by the court after conviction. Sentences can include fines, probation, probation with special conditions, jail, or prison if convicted of a felony.

sentence disparity. A phenomenon associated with discretion and indeterminate sentencing wherein offenders receive or serve different sentences for essentially similar crimes. Determinate sentencing and reduction in judicial discretion are thought to reduce disparity (*See*: discretion).

serial murder. The murder of three or more persons over a period of more than 30 days. (*See*: mass murder; spree murder)

sexual deviations. Deviations such as exhibitionism and rape are penalized by law, but many other forms of sexual behavior are arbitrarily called deviant because they depart from what is considered normal by a society. Other behaviors sometimes termed deviations include individual frigidity or impotence, same-sex orientation, anal intercourse, cunnilingus, and fellatio. The line between what society terms normal and abnormal shifts with time. Deviation is a label applied at a given time, and does not imply a condemnation of everything so termed. Some authorities have suggested that sexual anomaly would be a preferable term.

shared monopoly. When four or fewer companies supply at least 50 percent of a particular market.

shock probation. A judicial practice whereby an offender who has been sent to prison is granted early release by the sentencing judge and placed on probation, usually of not less than 30 days or more than 120 days after being sent to the prison. The rationale is that the offender will be so "shocked" by the prison experience that he or she will never commit such an offense again.

short-run hedonism. A term used by Albert Cohen to describe the behavior of lower-class delinquent youth. Refers to immediate gratification, or a "live for the moment" lifestyle, in contrast to the middle-class value of deferred gratification.

simple assault (*See*: assault)

simultaneity. A reciprocal cause-and-effect relationship between two variables; for instance, sanctions by the criminal justice system may affect the crime rate, but the crime rate may also affect the sanctions that are meted out by the criminal justice system.

situational choice theory. A brand of rational choice theory that views criminal behavior as a function of choices and decisions made within a context of situational constraints and opportunities.

Skinner, B(urrhus) F(rederic) (1904-1990). American psychologist. Born in Susquehanna, Pa., he was most noted for his rigorous adherence to the principles of behaviorism as first elaborated by Watson. He contended that observable behavior is the only appropriate object of study for psychology, whose purpose is to describe the conditions under which behavior is modified (learning), not to explain why this occurs. He studies behavior within the framework of conditioning.

One of Skinner's most important contributions was the distinction between classical Pavlovian conditioning, in which behavior is elicited (for example, reflex), and operant conditioning, in which behavior is emitted. Skinner's most controversial ideas are presented in his best selling books *Walden Two*, a utopian novel based on behavioristic engineering, and *Beyond Freedom and Dignity*, a call for a radical transformation of the way an individual views himself or herself and the problems faced in society.

social bond. The rather intangible link between individuals and the society in which they coexist. The social bond is created through the process of socialization.

social class. Distinctions made between individuals and groups of individuals on the basis of important defining social characteristics.

social contract theory. The French philosopher Jean Jacques Rousseau articulated the concept of "social contract" theory. He explained the social contract as a set of rules that guarantee life, liberty, and happiness to all citizens. The social contract is an agreement among the citizens of a country to form a civilized society and to establish an authority to make and enforce laws. The kind of laws established is based on the contract. In order to encourage compliance, the laws must have sanctions (penalties) attached to them. The belief that societies need laws from the outset so that the strongest members will not take control and impose their collective will on the weaker ones. Individuals born into such an arrangement automatically assume the contract. As part of this contract, citizens give up some freedoms in return for the security and tranquility provided by the law. Rousseau felt that government is a necessary evil because the population(s) need guidance in the exercise of their freedom. He asserted that the government should always be viewed with suspicion and that the less government the better. According to Rousseau, the government should always be completely dependent on the will of the people.

social constraint. A type of negative social control exercised by authority on behalf of the community. An example is subjecting offenders to custody, or limitation of freedom, or fines of sufficient rigor to prevent the repetition of offenses.

social control. The sum total of the processes whereby society, or any subgroup within it, secures conformity to the expectations of its constituent units, individuals, or groups. It exhibits two main forms: (1) coercive control and (2) persuasive control.

    Coercive control emanates from legislated sanctions enforced by the agencies of law and government accomplished by force or the threat of force. The types of behavior specifically designated for coercive control fall under the general category of crime.

    Persuasive control operates through all the various agencies and techniques that induce individuals to respond to the standards, wishes, and imperatives of the larger social group. The law is the most concrete, explicit, and obvious instrument of social control but by no means the most powerful or comprehensive. The greater bulk of social control falls in the persuasive category.

social control theory. Rather than stressing causative factors in criminal behavior, this perspective asks why people obey rules instead of breaking them. This theory addresses two types of social control—internal and external.

social construction of crime. The assumption of interactionists that the definition of "crime" and who is a "criminal" are products of a selection process by authorities in society.

social disorganization theory. A condition of norm ambiguity said to exist when a group is faced with social change, uneven development of culture, maladaptiveness, disharmony, conflict, and lack of consensus that contribute to increased crime and delinquency.

social epidemiology. The study of social epidemics and diseases of the social order.

social interactionists. Scholars who view the human self as formed through a process of social interaction.

social inequality. Occurs when some people have more power, influence and wealth than others. In social structure theory, inequality is directly related to the frustration felt by the lower classes when they do not have the means to attain their legitimate goals. The frustration felt by the lower classes can lead to resentment, bitterness, and tension, which in turn contributes to violence and criminality. Such inequality is generally inherent in the makeup of society and hence it is most often found in social structure theories. In sociology, the problems of social inequality are studies within the subdiscipline of social stratification.

socialization. The process whereby a person acquires values, attitudes, and behaviors in interaction with others. Significant others, especially parents, contribute the most to this role identity process. The socialization process is a major explanation for crime causation theories like differential association and differential reinforcement theory (*See*: social learning).

social injustice. The perception that the "haves" of society exercise undue power, influence and control over the "have nots."

social isolation. The feeling of rejection, loneliness or distancing from peers or the community at large. A sense of not belonging to a group and a belief that no one cares about your well-being.

social justice. The intelligent cooperation of people in producing an organically united community, so that every member has an equal and real opportunity to grow and learn to live to the best of his or her native abilities. These ideal conditions of justice through social union are essentially those of democracy. They may be summarized as follows: (a) for every child a normal birth, a healthy environment, abundant, good food and liberal, appropriate education; (b) for every mature person a secure job adapted to abilities; (c) for all persons an income adequate to maintain them efficiently in the position of their highest social service; and (d) for all persons such influence with the authorities that their needs and ideas receive due consideration.

social laws. Formulations of uniformities of social behavior under similar conditions, the validity of which has been tested by repeated observations and by various logical methods. Contemporary criminologists and sociologists have been less confident in announcing social laws, most of which have turned out to be unverified social theories, or, at most, social principles.

social learning theory. A psychological perspective that asserts that people learn how to behave by modeling themselves after others whom they have the opportunity to observe.

social legislation. Laws designed to improve and protect the economic and social position of those groups in society that, because of age, sex, race, physical, or mental defect, or lack of economic power (Civil Rights and Americans with Disabilities Acts), cannot achieve healthful and decent living standards for themselves. The term social legislation was coined by Wilhelm I of Germany in 1881 in a famous speech before the Reichstag urging the adoption of public accident and health insurance.

social pathology. A concept that compares society to a physical organism and sees criminality as an illness (*See*: medical model).

social problems perspective. The belief that crime is a manifestation of underlying social problems, such as poverty, discrimination, depressed living conditions, pervasive family violence, inadequate socialization practices, and the breakdown of traditional social institutions.

social process theories or **interactionist perspectives.** This concept emphasizes the give-and-take which occurs between offender, victim, and society and specifically between the offender and agents of formal social control, such as the criminal justice system: police, courts, and correctional organizations. Includes theories based on learning principles.

social psychology. The study of individuals in their social context and of the interactions of individuals in groups. Social psychologists build theories, as well as attempting to ameliorate immediate problems, such as misunderstandings between police and the community or the phenomenon of urban riots.

social reform. The general movement, or any specific result of that movement, that attempts to eliminate or mitigate the evils that result from the malfunctioning of the social system, or any part of it. In its concept and scope, social reform lies somewhere between social work and social engineering. It goes beyond the alleviation of individual and family hardship, usually the focus of social work, but it does not aim at the sweeping changes in social structure that are involved in social engineering. Social reform is closely affiliated with the ideas of social progress that characterized 19th-century thought in Western culture. It accepted the existing framework of society and sought to correct the ills associated with it. There have been numerous reform movements, such as expansion of the electorate, protection of the less powerful elements in society, and control of vice.

social relativity. The concept that social events are differently interpreted according to the cultural experiences and personal interests of the initiator, the observer, or the recipient of that behavior.

social responsibility. A view that holds that individuals are fundamentally responsible for their own behavior, and which maintains that they choose crime over other, more law-abiding courses of action (*See*: rational choice theory; classical theory).

social sanction. Any threat of penalty or promise of reward established by or for a group on the conduct of its members, to induce conformity to its rules or laws. Legal sanction is a form of social sanction, but the phrase may also be used to indicate any group sanctions other than legal.

social learning theory. A theory of crime which maintains that delinquent behavior is learned through the same psychological process as non-delinquent behavior, e.g., through reinforcement and modeling (*See:* differential association; differential reinforcement theory).

social-structural theories. These theories have their roots at the University of Chicago, Department of Sociology in about 1915. Robert Ezra Park began his study of urban life in the city of Chicago. Park and his colleague Burgess came to believe that behavior is controlled by social or ecological forces. Essentially, this theory holds that the social structure or the makeup of American society results in what they describe as natural areas, some of wealth and others of poverty. The natural areas of poverty are inevitably contained within the inner city which results in disintegration which then contributes to crime and delinquency. The focus of this school of thought is on lower-class crime, because in their view the conditions present in the slum and inner city are conducive to deviant behavior. There are three often overlapping branches of social structure theories: Social Disorganization Theory, strain theory, and Cultural Deviance Theory.

These theories explain crime by reference to the various aspects of the social fabric. They emphasize relationships among social institutions, and also describe the types of behavior that tend to characterize groups of people as opposed to individuals.

social structure. The pattern of social organization and the interrelationships between institutional characteristics of a society.

socialist school of criminology. As socialist thought developed in the early 20th century, scholars influenced by Marx) began to explain crime in terms of the exploitation of workers in capitalistic societies, a condition that, they contended, led to endemic poverty and misery, producing numerous criminal responses ranging from alcoholism and prostitution to larceny. The Marxists held that the legal system in capitalistic societies protected exploitive interests of the ruling-owner class, and that only reorganization of the economic order along socialist lines would prevent criminality.

society. A group of human beings cooperating in the pursuit of several of their major interests, invariably including self-maintenance and self-perpetuation. The concept of society includes continuity, complex associational relationships, and representatives of all fundamental types: men, women, and children. Ordinarily, there is also the element of territorial establishment. Society is a functioning group, so it is frequently defined in terms of relationships or processes. It is the basic, large-scale human group, sharply differentiated from fortuitous temporary or non-representative groups or aggregations such as a mob, the passengers on a cruise, or the spectators at a sporting event.

sociobiology. The systematic study of the biological basis of all social behavior.

socioeconomic. A demographic term which measures relative income.

sociology. A term first used by Auguste Comte (1798-1857), who attempted to outline a new discipline modeled on the natural sciences. The scientific study of the phenomena arising out the group relations of human beings; the study of humans and their environment in relation to each other. Different schools of sociology lay varying emphasis on the related factors, some stressing the relationships themselves, such as interaction and association; others emphasize human beings in their social relationships, focusing on the individual in varying roles and functions. Whether sociology, as currently developed, is entitled to the rank of a science is still a matter of some disagreement, but it is uniformly recognized that the methods of sociology may be strictly scientific, and that the verified generalizations that are the earmark of true science are being progressively built up out of extensive and painstaking observations and analysis of the repetitious uniformities in group behavior.

sociopath. An individual with a character disorder; an antisocial personality. (*See:* psychopath)

sociopathic personality disturbance. A disorder characteristic of chronically antisocial persons who seem unable or unwilling to live within established social and moral frameworks and who do not form stable and intimate interpersonal relationships. The primary concern of such individuals is the immediate gratification of their own needs and desires, and they show no interest in the effect their behavior may have on other persons or groups. Their actions are irresponsible and often destructive, yet they experience no guilt in the face of repeated recriminations. They often construct elaborate rationalizations that make their behavior seem acceptable and even necessary. (*See:* psychopath)

sociotherapy. A treatment method that usually attempts to modify those stressful conditions in a patient's life situation that are interfering with his or her adjustment. Increasing attention is being paid to alleviating destructive, dysfunctional or unhealthy family interactions, which involves treatment of two or more members of the family unit in addition to the original patient, or family therapy.

somatotyping. The classification of human beings into types according to body build and other physical characteristics. This school of thought asserts that such a classification relates to behavioral tendencies such as temperament, susceptibility to delinquency and disease, and life expectancy. William Sheldon developed three descriptive categories: the *endomorph* is round, soft, and smooth-skinned with short arms and legs; the *ectomorph* is thin-skinned, narrow, and slightly muscled with long arms and legs; and the *mesomorph* has large bones, very developed muscles, and thick skin. Most individuals are mixtures of all three types but can be rated in each category. Sheldon found that persons rated high in endomorphy tend to be relaxed, sociable, comfort-loving, and tolerant; those high in ectomorphy are often physically inhibited, secretive, and like intellectual activity; and those tending toward mesomorphy are more adventurous, aggressive, and like exercise. Applying his theory to 260 delinquent boys he found the mesomorphic type most disposed to delinquency, but there was not a one-to-one relationship. Sheldon believed this relationship emphasized the genetic influence on behavior; however, behavior influences physique as well. Each may spring from a common environmental cause.

Sorokin, Pitirim A. (1889-1969). Sociological thinker, a native of Russia, and a refugee from its 1917 revolution. He was a professor at Harvard University for many years. His prolific writing include *Crime and Punishment, Heroic Act and Reward* (1914), *Social Mobility* (1917), and *Social and Cultural Dynamics* (1941).

Spear, Charles (1801-1863). A Boston Universalist minister and an advocate of prison reform and the abolition of capital punishment, Spear helped organize the Society for the Abolition of Capital Punishment in 1844. He published *The Hangman* (1845), which the next year became *The Prisoner's Friend*, and was published through 1859. He and his brother John M. Spear, also a Universalist minister who later became a spiritualist, worked together to help discharge prisoners and pioneered in what ultimately became parole methods.

spiritual (religious) explanations. Positions that make use of other worldly powers to account for what happens. In criminology, and other social disciplines, rational scientific contemporary thought has dismissed the spiritual approach as a viable frame of reference (*See:* natural explanations).

spree murder. The killing of three or more people within 30 days. Often associated with felony homicides.

Spurzheim, Johann Kasper (1776-1832). After working in Europe, he brought the concept of phrenology to America. He suggested that individual personality traits are directly related to the conformations of their heads.

star chamber proceeding. A secret proceeding in which a person is given little or no opportunity to present his or her case or defense, and in which the proceedings are conducted and conclusions reached without observing usual judicial formalities. The term comes from the Star Chamber, an English court established by King Charles I and abolished by Parliament in 1641. The Star Chamber had no jury and was permitted to apply torture.

stare decisis. A Latin term meaning literally, "let the decision stand." This legal doctrine is the basis for case law. For example, one would judge the merits of a case predicated on a previously decided similar case.

status crime. May be referred to as status offenses. Generally applies to juveniles and involves behavior that would not be considered a crime if committed by an adult. Status offenses include truancy, running-away, incorrigibility, curfew violations, and the purchase or consumption of alcohol.

stereotype. The image held of one group by another or one person of another that is usually not supported by fact or documentation. Also, a rigid mental image of what is believed to be true about a particular group. An example would be "type casting" for a movie or television series.

stigma. A negative label which, according to Labeling Theory, can result in a self-fulfilling prophecy of further delinquency (*See*: self-fulfilling prophecy; Becker, Howard).

Stockholm syndrome. A term for misplaced empathy or compassion experienced by victims of terrorists, who may tend to identify with their captors or abductors, as was the case with a group held captive in a bank vault in Stockholm.

Stone, Lucy (1818-1893). Feminist, abolitionist, suffragette, and an agitator for women's rights. Married to abolitionist Henry B. Blackwell in 1855 in a ceremony that protested current marriage laws, she insisted on keeping her maiden name and was called "Mrs. Stone." After the Civil War, she participated in the American Equal Rights Association, and in 1869, became a leader of the American Woman Suffrage Association.

strain theory or **anomie theory.** A sociological approach of Structural theory which posits a disjuncture between socially and subculturally sanctioned means and goals as the cause of criminal behavior. The feelings of "strain" contribute to crime and delinquency. These theories tend to focus on the lower classes since it is precisely this group that often lacks the motivation or means to attain success in a materially oriented capitalistic society (*See:* Emile Durkheim; Robert Merton).

straw theory. A term used to describe the oversimplification of an existing theory.

Structural Marxism. The belief in Marxist theory that although the development of the law may be explained in capitalistic terms, the law does not always serve the best interests of the wealthy and powerful (*See*: conflict theory).

subcultural theory. A branch of Social Structure Theory that is most frequently associated with the work of Albert Cohen, author of *Delinquent Boys* (1955). Cohen believed that the delinquent behavior of lower-class youth was the result of the predominance of middle-class values in the United States. Cohen discussed "middle-class measuring rods" which put lower-class youth at a distinct disadvantage because they are socialized in the culture of the lower-class whose values often conflict with those of the middle-class. The inability to measure up to middle-class standards results in a rejection of these values. Instead, lower-class values like short-run hedonism and group autonomy are sought. In addition, Cohen believes that lower-class youth, unable to succeed by middle-class standards become frustrated and resort to a type of "reaction-formation" behavior that is in opposition to the middle-class standards they are unable to meet. Therefore, Cohen describes lower-class delinquent behavior as a "rebellion" against middle-class expectations. Subcultural theory holds that social forces are at the root of delinquent behavior. This perspective emphasizes the contribution made by variously socialized cultural groups to the phenomenon of crime.

subculture. A collection of values, attitudes and behaviors that are communicated to subcultural participants through a process of socialization.

sublimation. The psychological process whereby one aspect of consciousness comes to be symbolically substituted for another.

sub rosa. Not in public view; hidden; covert (not necessarily illegal).

suicide. To take one's own life. In some jurisdictions, this act is still a violation of the legal code. In early English law, those individuals committing suicide forfeited all property to the crown and lost the privilege to be buried in sanctified ground.

The classic work on suicide was done by Emile Durkheim in 1897. Durkheim found that suicide tended to be caused by social rather than psychological factors in that rates varied from one group to another. Protestants and city dwellers committed suicide at a higher rater than Catholics and people who lived in more rural communities. Those who lived alone also tended to commit suicide at a higher rate than those living with others. Durkheim focused on the extent to which people were isolated from their community. Those who have an extended social network tend to be insulated from life's pressures, whereas those who do not possess these social networks are more prone to commit suicide.

anomic. A suicide that occurs in a time of economic change when the individual experiences a dramatic change in life-style and is thrown into an unfamiliar and personally unsatisfying way of life.

superego. The moral aspect of the personality; much like the conscience. More formally, the division of the psyche that develops by the incorporation of the perceived moral standards of the community, is mainly unconscious, and includes the conscience.

Sutherland, Edwin H. (1883-1950). One of the most prominent of the current sociological-criminological theories of crime causation is the differential-association theory, first published in 1939 by Sutherland. The concept of crime as learned behavior had been formulated earlier (1890) by Gabriel Tarde. Sutherland began with this concept and formulated nine basic correlates in explaining the process by which a particular person comes to engage in criminal behavior. Criminality is explained in terms of the environment. All criminal behavior is learned, and to determine whether a person is likely to commit a deviant act, one needs to balance criminal associations against noncriminal associations of the individual person. The balance, however, must be a sophisticated one, including such variables as frequency, duration, priority, and intensity. (*See:* Tarde, Gabriel)

symbolic interaction. An explanation of behavior derived from sociology, which contends that people communicate through symbols. The major symbol of interaction in any society is language and we come to interpret our behavior thought these symbols in interaction with others.

synomie. A societal state, opposite of anomie, marked by social cohesion achieved through the sharing of common values.

T

Tarde, Gabriel (1843-1904). French jurist, philosopher, psychologist, sociologist, as well as a criminologist of international repute. The concept of crime as learned behavior was formulated by Tarde, who in 1890 published his ideas in his *Laws of Imitation.* His emphasis on the social origins of crime is a cornerstone of present American criminological theories. His devastating attack on the Lombrosian Theory undermined the influence of that school in Europe. In the field of penology, Tarde provided a theory of moral responsibility that was original and capable of practical demonstration.

target hardening. A crime prevention approach to reduce criminal opportunity. Generally through the use of physical barriers, architectural design, and enhanced security measures (lighting, dogs, patrols) of a particular location.

taxonomy. The science or technique of classification.

team policing. A decentralized method of policing popularized in the 1970s that uses a self-contained group of officers who are permanently assigned to a particular zone or community.

techniques of neutralization. Developed by Matza who believed that delinquents use neutralizations or rationalizations to excuse their illegal behavior thereby allowing them to drift back and forth from conforming to nonconforming behavior (*See*: social process theory).

terrorism. The use of violence against a target to create fear, alarm, dread, or coercion for the purpose of obtaining concessions or rewards or commanding public attention for a political cause.

testosterone. The most abundant male sex hormone which is produced in the testes and controls secondary sex characteristics, such as facial hair and voice level. Research has found that abnormally high levels of testosterone contribute to higher levels of aggression and violence. A study by L.E. Kreuz and R.M. Rose in 1972, asserted that testosterone levels were higher in prisoner populations who committed crimes of violence than in other prisoners whose crimes did not involve violence.

thanatology. The study of the theories, conditions, and causes of death. This term derives from Thanotos, an ancient Greek personification of death. Except for its use in the medical term, thanatosis," which refers to the appearance of death of an organism or part of the body, this archaic reference is most frequently found in literary materials.

theoretical range. The levels or scope of analysis that may serve as an explanation of a theory.

theoretical system. The systematic combinations of taxonomies (classifications), conceptual frameworks, descriptors, explanations, and predictions that provide structure for the support of an empirical phenomenon.

theory. A series of interrelated propositions that attempt to describe, explain, predict, and ultimately to control some class of events. A theory gains explanatory power from inherent logical consistency, and is "tested" by how well it describes and predicts reality.

threat analysis or **risk analysis.** This involves a complete and thorough assessment of the kinds of internal and external perils facing an organization.

Tocqueville, (Charles) Alexis de (1805-1858). French political theorist whose work, *Democracy in America,* remains one of the most penetrating analyses ever written of United States institutions and national character. In 1831, Tocqueville was sent to the United States for a year to study the prison system. On his return to France, he coauthored a study of U.S. prisons, which was followed in 1835 by the first parts of *Democracy in America.*

tradition. Custom that has been handed down from one generation to another.

transportation. A method of punishment originally devised in England for individuals classified as "criminals." It had a precedent in the practice of outlawry, whereby certain persons could escape hanging by becoming exiles. When the American Revolution put an end to the practice there, England began transporting convicts to Australia, New Zealand, and Van Diemen's Land (Tasmania). Between 1790 and 1840 it was reported that Australia accepted 75,000 convicts. Prisoners were also transported by czarist Russia to Siberia, and by France to Devil's Island.

trephination. A form of surgery, typically involving bone and especially the skull. Early instances of cranial trephination have been taken as evidence for primitive beliefs in spirit possession.

trial by ordeal. An old criminal justice proceeding in which the innocence of a defendant was tested by being thrown into cold water. If the person sank, a verdict of innocent would be rendered. If the person floated, guilty. If the person could walk blindfolded and unharmed over red hot irons or drink with impunity the most deadly poisons, the person was considered innocent.

tutelage. Instruction or socialization in criminal motives and skills, including how to recognize criminal opportunity, how to plan, and how to accomplish.

twelve tables. Early Roman laws, written approximately 450 B.C., that regulated family, religious and economic life.

twins. (*See*: concordance rate)

Type A personality. A personality profile which is believed to lead to stress and heart disease. People who show Type A behavior tend to be competitive, hostile, impatient individuals who are constantly under stress. People who show

Type B behavior tend to be able to react to environmental demands and to deal with stress effectively.

U

uni-causal. Means having one cause. Theories that are uni-causal posit only one source for all that they attempt to explain.

urban. Refers to city life.

urban vigilantism. The increasing tendency for large metropolitan residents to arm themselves to enforce the law, protect themselves, and battle crime due to the perception that organized law enforcement agencies are not able to protect them. Vigilantism is based on the belief (self-survival) that it is permissible to take the law into one's own hand(s) if the cause is just. The New York subway vigilante, Bernhard H. Goetz, is perhaps the best example of this behavior.

urbanization. The development of densely populated communities. The creation of business or industry in geographically confined areas.

urban renewal. The removal of deteriorated properties and new construction of buildings, businesses and communities.

underground economy. Unreported, untaxed, unregulated, and often illegal economic transactions that take place outside of the official and legal economy. This practice is often termed "barter economy."

unjust law. This is a contradiction of terms for traditional criminologists but not so for civil libertarians. According to Martin Luther King, Jr., a law is unjust if it (a) compels a minority to obey but is not binding on the majority, (b) is unfair to a minority that was denied the right to vote on it, and (c) is fair but unjust in its application.

usury. Interest that exceeds legal limitations.

utilitarianism. A political philosophy based on the principle of the "the greatest good for the greatest number." The concept was developed by the British philosopher Jeremy Bentham, who based it on the principle that pleasure was preferable to pain. Public policy ought to be aimed at what he termed maximum utility—that is, the maximization of pleasure for the maximum number of citizens. Any proposed policy—in politics, law, or economics—could in principle be measured in terms of its utility.

Bentham recognized that few if any proposals would have a general utility, and that some citizens would always be adversely affected by particular policies, but he proposed the use of a "felicific or hedonistic calculus" to weigh the extent of pleasure and pain involved in specific cases. This notion has been ridiculed on the grounds that no objective assessment of utility is possible. The utilitarian principle of seeking to maximize good in public policies has been influential, however, particularly in economic theory.

V

values. A value is an enduring belief that a specific mode of conduct or behavior is personally or socially preferable to other choices. Value-programming can be divided into three periods: (1) imprinting, which occurs during the first six to seven years of age, in addition to physical behavior development, a tremendous amount of mental development takes place; (2) modeling, generally takes place from seven or eight to 13 or 14 years of age, the process of identification—initially with the parents and significant others; and (3) socialization, which occurs from 13 or 14 to around 20 years of age. This is when our social life becomes structured primarily in terms of friends and peer groups.

Values, while enduring, can be altered. This change can occur by (1) a traumatic or significant emotional event, or (2) by a profound dissatisfaction.

value conflict. This is a significant factor in explaining delinquency from a sociological perspective. Specifically, social structure theory holds that children who are raised in impoverished slum areas develop values that are different from middle-class norms, which expect strict compliance with the law. When these values clash or are in conflict, the lower-class adolescent often finds himself or herself in violation of the law (*See*: social disorganization; strain theory; cultural deviance theory).

variables. Changeable factors.

vandalism. The destroying or damaging, or attempting to destroy or damage, the property of another without his or her consent, except by burning, which is arson.

victimization rate. A measure of the occurrence of victimization among a specified population group. For personal crimes, this is based on the number of victimizations per 1,000 residents age 12 or older. For household crimes, the victimization rates are calculated using the number of incidents per 1,000 households.

victimization survey. A systematic effort to measure the experiences of the victims of crime by interviewing a cross section of a population.

victimless crimes. These crimes represent behaviors that have been outlawed because they conflict with the norms and values of contemporary society. These laws are controversial because they prohibit behavior which tends to be widespread and often committed by adults and arguably without injury to others. These are crimes that generally do not have a complaining victim such as gambling, drug use, pornography, deviant sex acts and prostitution.

victimogenesis. The contributory background of a victim as a result of which that individual becomes prone to victimization.

victimology. The study of the psychological and dynamic interrelationships between victims and offenders, with a view toward crime prevention. Interest in the study of the victim arose in the 1940s, and the works of such scholars as Mendelsohn (1947) and Von Hentig (1948) underlined the importance of studying criminal-victim relationships in understanding crime.

violent crimes. Serious crimes, such as murder, robbery and rape, committed against people, in contrast to property crimes like theft and vandalism.

vitamin deficiencies. This theory holds that if people do not receive the proper level of nutrition they will suffer vitamin deficiency, which could be manifested in mental and behavioral problems. A number of problems have been associated with vitamin deficiency including depression, agitation, memory loss, cognitive problems and aggression.

Vold, George Bryan (1896-1967). George B. Vold, the son of Norwegian immigrants, was born in South Dakota. He received his master's degree in sociology from the University of Chicago in 1924 and completed his doctoral work at the University of Minnesota, receiving his Ph.D. in 1930. A few years later he became a full professor at Minnesota, where he spent his entire academic career. He studied the Massachusetts prison system, returned to Minnesota to serve on the state's Crime Commission and wrote important works on parole and police training. He was the author of *Theoretical Criminology* (1958), which became the leading book in the field. In 1966, The American Society of Criminology bestowed on him the prestigious Edwin Sutherland Award.

Vollmer, August (1876-1955). Vollmer began his distinguished law enforcement career in 1905, when he was elected town marshal for the city of Berkeley, California. He assisted in the creation of the State Bureau of Criminal Identification, and he promoted a police school in conjunction with the University of California, San Jose, in 1916. He was appointed Professor of Police Administration at the University of Chicago in 1929, accepting full professorship at the University of California in 1931. Vollmer introduced the bicycle for patrol, radio-equipped police cars, and implemented the police telephone or the call box system. During his career, he served as a consultant to survey and reorganize police departments in 75 American and foreign cities. He inaugurated the use of automatic tabulating machinery to marshal the facts of crime and established the first scientific crime-detection laboratory. He is considered the Father of Modern American Police and the Dean of American Police Chiefs.

Voltaire, Francois Marie Arouet (1694-1778). One of the world's greatest philosophers, this Frenchman recommended that there be a reduction of the death and infamy punishments, a means of making all penalties more socially useful, and a legislature free of outside influences. Voltaire stated that only those acts that are contrary to society's survival should be considered criminal and that all punishments should be proportional to the crime committed.

voyeurism. The surreptitious viewing of another for sexual gratification.

W

Walnut Street Jail. The development of the penitentiary started with the Walnut Street Jail in Philadelphia in 1790. A part of this facility was altered to conform with the principles of separate confinement or complete isolation.

war on drugs. A declaration made during the Bush administration that stated the policy of the United States as it pertained to the eradication of drugs in our society. The "war" has been the subject of much controversy and speculation by many when referring to the effectiveness of controlling the use and sale of drugs in the United States. This strategy attempts to control drugs through aggressive enforcement, mandatory minimums, and punishment.

war on poverty. This was a social policy implemented during the administration of Lyndon B. Johnson in the 1960s. The war on poverty was influenced by social structural theories of crime and delinquency, which concluded that increased opportunities afforded to those segments of society that experience poverty and discrimination will reduce the myriad of social problems present in American society. Although this policy continues to be a subject of debate, most criminologists agree that it had a negligible effect on crime rates.

Watson, John Broadus (1878-1958). American psychologist born in Greenville, S.C. Watson fathered what has come to be known as the "behaviorist revolt." He rejected the then-popular trend of studying such matters as mental activity and conscious experience, arguing that concepts of that sort belong in the realm of philosophy. They have no place in an objective science because there is no way of directly observing or objectively measuring them. He declared that psychology should be limited to the study of behavior and should concern itself especially with stimulus-response connections, which he called habit formation. Given the stimulus connections, the psychologist should be able to predict the response. It was Watson who claimed that if given full charge of 12 healthy infants, he could, by means of behavioral conditioning, produce any type of person he desired - doctor lawyer, or even criminal.

Weber, Max (1864-1920). This German sociologist had a major impact on Western sociology and criminology. His many and varied writings covered politics, law, economics, music, cities, and world religions. Much of Weber's work is considered a response to the position of Karl Marx. Marx believed that societies would move more toward social equality but Weber did not necessarily welcome this change because he felt it meant a greater level of intrusiveness by the state over the rights of the individual. Unlike Marx, he did not feel that the structure of society and social change were inevitably tied to economic factors. Instead, he believed that religious thought played a critical factor. In sociology, Weber took the lead in arguing that study and investigation should be value-free or without personal bias.

wergeld. A medieval term for the worth of a person injured by another according to the victim's station in society.

Wergeld was the amount of compensation the offender was compelled to pay either the victim or a representative in order to resolve the difficulty. If the wergeld was not paid, private retaliation could then be exercised against the offender and kin by the victim and his or her family.

white-collar crime. Those criminal acts typically associated with persons involved in "white-collar" occupations (e.g., embezzlement). "Blue-collar" is generally a term used to describe the work force laborers.

Wilson, Orlando Winfield (1900-1972). A police reformer who has often been credited with the promotion of police professionalism. Wilson learned police reform while a patrolman under August Vollmer at Berkeley, California, in 1921. He was police chief in Wichita, Kansas, in 1928 and convinced the Kansas League of Municipalities to create a statewide police training school in 1931 and to appoint him the director. He drafted the Square Deal Code of Wichita, which was later adopted as a code of ethics by the International Association of Chiefs of Police. By 1939, Wilson had achieved national prominence, but he had also irritated too many Wichita politicians. He resigned as Chief of Police and accepted a professorship in police administration at the University of California, Berkeley, and founded the first professional school of criminology there after World War II ended. As dean, Wilson became an extremely influential reformer. Wilson was appointed Chief of Police of Chicago in 1960 and retired in 1967.

Wines, Enoch Cobb (1806-1879). As secretary of the New York Prison Association from 1862 and until his death, Wines was the guiding force of American corrections. He was central to organizing the National Prison Association. In 1872, he served as the U.S. representative to the 26-nation International Penitentiary Congress. He resigned as president of the City University of St. Louis in 1862 to enter the prison reform movement. Wines expounded the ties of education, religion, and penology during the latter part of the nineteenth century. His 1880 book, *The State of Prisons and of Child-Saving Institutions in the Civilized World*, asserted that religion was paramount to productive life and that moral forces should replace physical forces. He felt that a "wretched homelife or lack of homelife" was a significant source of criminal behavior.

Wolfgang, Marvin. Criminologist best known for his 1972 Philadelphia Birth Cohort Study, which identified the chronic offender.

work release. A legal decision whereby an inmate in a correctional setting is allowed to work in the community during the day and return to the correctional facility at night or on weekends.

X

XYY chromosomal aberration. A physical trait of an unusual chromosome pattern. Some scholars claimed the extra "Y" could cause men to become overly aggressive and prone to violence, and because it was an inherited trait, it might explain and in some cases, excuse behavior (*See*: genetics).

Y

youth culture. A distinctive subculture consisting of young people whose norms, values, and roles differ significantly from those of the surrounding society. Youth cultures exist in all but a few small-scale preliterate societies, but the degree to which each is differentiated from the main culture varies.

The existence of such subcultures is a taken-for-granted part of American social reality. Yet the term "adolescent" was popularized in America only in 1904 by the psychologist G. Stanley Hall, and it was not until the years preceding World War I that the existence of a distinctive but problematic age group—those who had passed puberty but were denied adult responsibilities—was recognized. More recently, Kenneth Keniston has suggested the incorporation of another stage into the life cycle, that between adolescence and adulthood. He terms this emergent period *youth,* and suggests that it runs from the ages of 18 to about 30; its members are "post-adolescent yet preadult."

The most distinctive form of youth culture in the United States in recent decades is that which has been termed the counterculture. Strongly influenced by "hippie" values and attitudes toward dress, work, sexual behavior, and property, this youth subculture created considerable sociological and criminological attention. Its members tended to be white and middle class in origin, and their apparent rejection of mainstream values was held by some observers to portend major social change in the United States. However, the increasingly conservative tendencies of young people in the 1980s, at least on political and economic if not social issues, and the rising importance of material attainment led scholars to doubt that youth possessed any special radical potential.

The conventional young still, of course, form a youth culture. They have their own heroes, jargon, and leisure activities, which are not shared by adult society. But such differences may represent little more that the marginal generational discontinuity that might be expected in times of rapid social change.

A third form of youth culture is that of delinquent groups. Members of delinquent subcultures tend to be drawn from lower-class or working-class backgrounds, and their delinquency is often a response to the realization that their future social roles will most likely be unrewarding. Their school curriculum is seen as irrelevant, and their ultimate occupations are apt to be stultifying and poorly paid. Accordingly, interest is focused on the search for "kicks" and immediate gratification, even though these may take the form of illegal acts.

Z

zero tolerance. A political mandate asserting that even minute amounts of drugs or contraband are violations of the law and will result in full prosecution.

SOURCES AND RECOMMENDED READING

Adler, Freda,et. al., *Criminology*, McGraw-Hill, 1995.

Bailey, William G., *The Encyclopedia of Police Science*, Garland Publishing, 1995.

Conklin, John E., *Criminology*, 5th ed., Allyn and Bacon, 1995.

Einstadter, Werner and Stuart Henry, *Criminological Theory: An Analysis of Its Underlying Assumptions,* Harcourt Brace Javanovich Inc., 1995.

Ferrell, Jeff and Clinton R. Sanders, *Cultural Criminology,* Northeastern University Press, 1995.

Ross, Robert S., *American National Government: Institutions, Policy, and Participation*, 3rd ed., Dushkin Publishing Group, Inc., 1993.

Reid, Sue Titus, *Crime and Criminology* , 8th ed., Brown and Benchmark, 1997.

Rush, George E., *The Dictionary of Criminal Justice,* 4th ed., Dushkin Publishing Group, Inc., 1994.

Schmalleger, Frank, *Criminology Today*, Prentice-Hall, NJ., 1996.

Sykes, Gresham, and Francis T. Cullen, *Criminology,* 2nd ed., Harcourt Brace Javanovich Inc., 1992.

Vito, Gennaro F. and Ronald M. Holmes, *Criminology, Theory, Research, and Policy,* Wadsworth Publishing Co., 1994.

Walker, Samuel, *Sense and Nonsense About Crime and Drugs* 3rd ed., Wadsworth Publishing Company, 1994.